CALIFORNIA REVISED UNIFORM LIMITED LIABILITY COMPANY ACT

2015 Edition

As amended through January 1, 2015

Michigan Legal Publishing Ltd.
QUICK DESK REFERENCE SERIES™

© 2014, 2015 Michigan Legal Publishing Ltd.
Grand Rapids, Michigan

Academic and bulk discounts available at
www.michlp.com

No claim to copyright of any government works. While we make every effort to ensure this text is accurate, there is no guarantee that the rules and statutes in this publication are the latest and most up-to-date. Accordingly, this text is for educational purposes only and should not be considered legal advice.

WE WELCOME YOUR FEEDBACK: info@michlp.com

ISBN-13: 978-1505453874
ISBN-10: 1505453879

CALIFORNIA REVISED UNIFORM LIMITED LIABILITY COMPANY ACT

Contents

ARTICLE 1. General Provisions [17701.01 - 17701.17] 4
    17701.01. 4
    17701.02. 4
    17701.04. 7
    17701.05. 8
    17701.06. 9
    17701.07. 9
    17701.08. 10
    17701.09. 11
    17701.10. 11
    17701.11. 13
    17701.12. 13
    17701.13. 14
    17701.14. 15
    17701.15. 15
    17701.16. 16
    17701.17. 17

ARTICLE 2. Formation: Articles of Organization and Other Filings [17702.01 - 17702.10] 17
    17702.01. 17
    17702.02. 18
    17702.03. 19
    17702.04. 20
    17702.05. 21
    17702.06. 21
    17702.07. 22
    17702.09. 23
    17702.10. 24

ARTICLE 3. Relations of Members and Managers to Persons Dealing with a Limited Liability Company [17703.01 - 17703.04] 25
    17703.01. 25
    17703.04. 26

ARTICLE 4. Relations of Members to Each Other and to the Limited Liability Company [17704.01 - 17704.10] 27
    17704.01. 27
    17704.02. 27
    17704.03. 28
    17704.04. 28
    17704.05. 29
    17704.06. 30
    17704.07. 31
    17704.08. 37
    17704.09. 38

17704.10. 38

ARTICLE 5. Transferable Interests and Rights of Transferees and Creditors [17705.01 - 17705.04] 40

17705.01. 40
17705.02. 41
17705.03. 42
17705.04. 42

ARTICLE 6. Member's Dissociation [17706.01 - 17706.03] 43

17706.01. 43
17706.02. 43
17706.03. 45

ARTICLE 7. Dissolution and Winding Up [17707.01 - 17707.09] 45

17707.01. 45
17707.02. 46
17707.03. 47
17707.04. 48
17707.05. 49
17707.06. 49
17707.07. 50
17707.08. 51
17707.09. 52

ARTICLE 8. Foreign Limited Liability Companies [17708.01 - 17708.09] 53

17708.01. 53
17708.02. 53
17708.03. 54
17708.04. 55
17708.05. 56
17708.06. 57
17708.07. 57
17708.08. 57
17708.09. 58

ARTICLE 9. Actions by Members [17709.01 - 17709.02] 58

17709.01. 58
17709.02. 58

ARTICLE 10. Merger and Conversion [17710.01 - 17710.19] 60

17710.01. 60
17710.02. 61
17710.03. 62
17710.04. 63
17710.05. 64
17710.06. 64
17710.07. 65
17710.08. 66
17710.09. 67
17710.10. 69
17710.11. 69
17710.12. 69

17710.13.	72
17710.14.	72
17710.15.	74
17710.16.	75
17710.17.	75
17710.18.	77
17710.19.	77

ARTICLE 11. Dissenters' Rights [17711.01 - 17711.14] 78

17711.01.	78
17711.02.	78
17711.03.	79
17711.04.	80
17711.05.	81
17711.06.	81
17711.07.	82
17711.08.	82
17711.09.	83
17711.10.	83
17711.11.	83
17711.12.	84
17711.13.	84
17711.14.	84

ARTICLE 12. Class Provisions [17712.01- 17712.01.] 85

17712.01.	85

ARTICLE 13. Miscellaneous Provisions [17713.01 - 17713.13] 86

17713.01.	86
17713.02.	86
17713.03.	86
17713.04.	86
17713.05.	87
17713.06.	87
17713.07.	88
17713.08.	88
17713.09.	89
17713.10.	90
17713.11.	91
17713.12.	91
17713.13.	94

ARTICLE 1. General Provisions [17701.01 - 17701.17]

CALIFORNIA REVISED UNIFORM LIMITED LIABILITY COMPANY ACT

ARTICLE 1. General Provisions [17701.01 - 17701.17]

17701.01.

This title may be cited as the California Revised Uniform Limited Liability Company Act.

(Added by Stats. 2012, Ch. 419, Sec. 20. Effective January 1, 2013. Operative January 1, 2014, by Sec. 32 of Ch. 419.)

17701.02.

In this title:
(a) "Acknowledged" means that an instrument is either of the following:
   (1) Formally acknowledged as provided in Article 3 (commencing with Section 1180) of Chapter 4 of Title 4 of Part 4 of Division 2 of the Civil Code.
   (2) Executed to include substantially the following wording preceding the signature: "It is hereby declared that I am the person who executed this instrument which execution is my act and deed." Any certificate of acknowledgment taken without this state before a notary public or a judge or clerk of a court of record having an official seal need not be further authenticated.
(b) "Articles of organization" means the articles required by Section 17702.01. The term includes the articles of organization as amended or restated.
(c) "Contribution" means any benefit provided by a person to a limited liability company:
   (1) In order to become a member upon formation of the limited liability company and in accordance with an agreement between or among the persons that have agreed to become the initial members of the limited liability company.
   (2) In order to become a member after formation of the limited liability company and in accordance with an agreement between the person and the limited liability company.
   (3) In the person's capacity as a member and in accordance with the operating agreement or an agreement between the member and the limited liability company.
(d) "Debtor in bankruptcy" means a person that is the subject of either of the following:
   (1) An order for relief under Title 11 of the United States Code or a successor statute of general application.
   (2) A comparable order under federal, state, or foreign law governing bankruptcy or insolvency, an assignment for the benefit of creditors, or an order appointing a trustee, receiver, or liquidator of the person or of all or substantially all of the person's property.
(e) "Designated office" means either of the following:

(1) The office that a limited liability company is required to designate and maintain under Section 17701.13.
(2) The principal office of a foreign limited liability company.
(f) "Distribution," except as otherwise provided in subdivision (g) of Section 17704.05, means a transfer of money or other property from a limited liability company to another person on account of a transferable interest.
(g) "Domestic" means organized under the laws of this state when used in relation to any limited liability company, other business entity, or person other than a natural person.
(h) "Effective," with respect to a record required or permitted to be delivered to the Secretary of State for filing under this title, means effective under subdivision (c) of Section 17702.05.
(i)
(1) "Electronic transmission by the limited liability company" means a communication delivered by any of the following means:
   (A) Facsimile telecommunication or electronic mail when directed to the facsimile number or electronic mail address, respectively, for that recipient on record with the limited liability company.
   (B) Posting on an electronic message board or network that the limited liability company has designated for those communications, together with a separate notice to the recipient of the posting, which transmission shall be validly delivered upon the later of the posting or delivery of the separate notice thereof.
   (C) Other means of electronic communication to which both of the following apply:
      (i) The communication is delivered to a recipient who has provided an unrevoked consent to the use of those means of transmission.
      (ii) The communication creates a record that is capable of retention, retrieval, and review, and that may thereafter be rendered into clearly legible tangible form. However, an electronic transmission by a limited liability company to an individual member is not authorized unless, in addition to satisfying the requirements of this section, the transmission satisfies the requirements applicable to consumer consent to electronic records as set forth in the federal Electronic Signatures in Global and National Commerce Act (15 U.S.C. Sec. 7001(c)(1)).
(2) "Electronic transmission to the limited liability company" means a communication delivered by any of the following means:
   (A) Facsimile telecommunication or electronic mail when directed to the facsimile number or electronic mail address, respectively, that the limited liability company has provided from time to time to members or managers for sending communications to the limited liability company.
   (B) Posting on an electronic message board or network that the limited liability company has designated for those communications, which transmission shall be validly delivered upon the posting.

ARTICLE 1. General Provisions [17701.01 - 17701.17]

(C) Other means of electronic communication to which both of the following apply:
  (i) The limited liability company has placed in effect reasonable measures to verify that the sender is the member or manager, in person or by proxy, purporting to send the transmission.
  (ii) The communication creates a record that is capable of retention, retrieval, and review, and that may thereafter be rendered into clearly legible tangible form.

(j) "Foreign limited liability company" means an unincorporated entity formed under the law of a jurisdiction other than this state and denominated by that law as a limited liability company.

(k) "Limited liability company," except in the phrase "foreign limited liability company," means an entity formed under this title or an entity that becomes subject to this title pursuant to Article 13 (commencing with Section 17713.01).

(l) "Majority of the managers" unless otherwise provided in the operating agreement, means more than 50 percent of the managers of the limited liability company.

(m) "Majority of the members" unless otherwise provided in the operating agreement, means more than 50 percent of the membership interests of members in current profits of the limited liability company.

(n) "Manager" means a person that under the operating agreement of a manager-managed limited liability company is responsible, alone or in concert with others, for performing the management functions stated in subdivision (c) of Section 17704.07.

(o) "Manager-managed limited liability company" means a limited liability company that qualifies under subdivision (a) of Section 17704.07.

(p) "Member" means a person that has become a member of a limited liability company under Section 17704.01 and has not dissociated under Section 17706.02.

(q) "Member-managed limited liability company" means a limited liability company that is not a manager-managed limited liability company.

(r) "Membership interest" means a member's rights in the limited liability company, including the member's transferable interest, any right to vote or participate in management, and any right to information concerning the business and affairs of the limited liability company provided by this title.

(s) "Operating agreement" means the agreement, whether or not referred to as an operating agreement and whether oral, in a record, implied, or in any combination thereof, of all the members of a limited liability company, including a sole member, concerning the matters described in subdivision (a) of Section 17701.10. The term "operating agreement" may include, without more, an agreement of all members to organize a limited liability company pursuant to this title. An operating agreement of a limited liability company having only one member shall not be unenforceable by reason of there being only one person who is a party to the operating agreement. The term includes the agreement as amended or restated.

(t) "Organization" means, whether domestic or foreign, a partnership whether general or limited, limited liability company, association, corporation, professional corporation, professional association, nonprofit corporation, business trust, or statutory business trust having a governing statute.

(u) "Organizer" means a person that acts under Section 17702.01 to form a limited liability company.
(v) "Person" means an individual, partnership, limited partnership, trust, estate, association, corporation, limited liability company, or other entity, whether domestic or foreign. Nothing in this subdivision shall be construed to confer any rights under the California Constitution or the United States Constitution.
(w) "Principal office" means the principal executive office of a limited liability company or foreign limited liability company, whether or not the office is located in this state.
(x) "Record" means information that is inscribed on a tangible medium or that is stored in an electronic or other medium and is retrievable in perceivable form.
(y) "State" means a state of the United States, the District of Columbia, Puerto Rico, the United States Virgin Islands, or any territory or insular possession subject to the jurisdiction of the United States.
(z) "Transfer" includes an assignment, conveyance, deed, bill of sale, lease, mortgage, security interest, encumbrance, gift, and transfer by operation of law.
(aa) "Transferable interest" means the right, as originally associated with a person's capacity as a member, to receive distributions from a limited liability company in accordance with the operating agreement, whether or not the person remains a member or continues to own any part of the right.
(ab) "Transferee" means a person to which all or part of a transferable interest has been transferred, whether or not the transferor is a member.
(ac) "Vote" includes authorization by written consent or consent given by electronic transmission to the limited liability company.

(Added by Stats. 2012, Ch. 419, Sec. 20. Effective January 1, 2013. Operative January 1, 2014, by Sec. 32 of Ch. 419.)

17701.04.

(a) A limited liability company is an entity distinct from its members.
(b) A limited liability company may have any lawful purpose, regardless of whether for profit, except the banking business, the business of issuing policies of insurance and assuming insurance risks, or the trust company business. A domestic or foreign limited liability company may render services that may be lawfully rendered only pursuant to a license, certificate, or registration authorized by the Business and Professions Code, the Chiropractic Act, the Osteopathic Act, or the Yacht and Ship Brokers Act, if the applicable provisions of the Business and Professions Code, the Chiropractic Act, the Osteopathic Act, or the Yacht and Ship Brokers Act authorize a limited liability company or foreign limited liability company to hold that license, certificate, or registration.
(c) A limited liability company has perpetual duration.
(d) Notwithstanding subdivision (b) and as specifically provided in this subdivision, a limited liability company may operate as a health care service plan licensed pursuant to Chapter 2.2 (commencing with Section 1340) of Division 2 of the Health and Safety Code if the limited liability company is a subsidiary of a health care service plan licensed pursuant to those provisions and the limited liability company is

established to serve an existing line of business of the parent health care service plan. Notwithstanding any other law, the tort or contract liability of a limited liability company created to operate as a health care service plan under this subdivision and its members is not limited or restricted in any manner because of the limited liability company status of the health care service plan.
(e) Nothing in this title shall be construed to permit a domestic or foreign limited liability company to render professional services, as defined in subdivision (a) of Section 13401 and in Section 13401.3, in this state.

(Added by Stats. 2012, Ch. 419, Sec. 20. Effective January 1, 2013. Operative January 1, 2014, by Sec. 32 of Ch. 419.)

17701.05.

Subject to any limitations contained in the articles of organization and to compliance with this title and any other applicable laws, a limited liability company organized under this title shall have all the powers of a natural person in carrying out its business activities, including, without limitation, the power to:
(a) Transact its business, carry on its operations, qualify to do business, and have and exercise the powers granted by this title in any state, territory, district, possession, or dependency of the United States, and in any foreign country.
(b) Sue, be sued, complain, and defend any action, arbitration, or proceeding, whether judicial, administrative, or otherwise, in its own name.
(c) Adopt, use, and at will alter a company seal. However, failure to affix a seal does not affect the validity of any instrument.
(d) Make contracts and guarantees, incur liabilities, act as surety, or borrow money.
(e) Sell, lease, exchange, transfer, convey, mortgage, pledge, or otherwise dispose of all or any part of its property and assets.
(f) Purchase, take, receive, lease, or otherwise acquire, own, hold, improve, use, or otherwise deal in and with any interest in real or personal property, wherever located.
(g) Lend money to and otherwise assist its members and employees.
(h) Issue notes, bonds, and other obligations and secure any of them by mortgage or deed of trust or security interest of any or all of its assets.
(i) Purchase, take, receive, subscribe for, or otherwise acquire, own, hold, vote, use, employ, sell, mortgage, loan, pledge, or otherwise dispose of and otherwise use and deal in and with stock or other interests in and obligations of any person, or direct or indirect obligations of the United States or of any government, state, territory, governmental district, or municipality, or of any instrumentality of any of them.
(j) Invest its surplus funds, lend money from time to time in any manner which may be appropriate to enable it to carry on the operations or fulfill the purposes set forth in its articles of organization, or take and hold real property and personal property as security for the payment of funds so loaned or invested.
(k) Be a promoter, stockholder, partner, member, manager, associate, or agent of any person.
(l) Indemnify or hold harmless any person.
(m) Purchase and maintain insurance.

(n) Issue, purchase, redeem, receive, take, or otherwise acquire, own, hold, sell, lend, exchange, transfer, or otherwise dispose of, pledge, use, and otherwise deal in and with its own bonds, debentures, and other securities.
(o) Pay pensions and establish and carry out pension, profit sharing, bonus, share purchase, option, savings, thrift, and other retirement, incentive, and benefit plans, trusts, and provisions for all or any of the current or former members, managers, officers, or employees of the limited liability company or any of its subsidiary or affiliated entities, or to indemnify and purchase and maintain insurance on behalf of any fiduciary of those plans, trusts, or provisions.
(p) Make donations, regardless of specific benefit to the limited liability company, to the public welfare or for community, civic, religious, charitable, scientific, literary, educational, or similar purposes.
(q) Make payments or donations or do any other act, not inconsistent with this title or any other applicable law, that furthers the business and affairs of the limited liability company.
(r) Pay compensation, and pay additional compensation, to any or all managers, officers, members, and employees on account of services previously rendered to the limited liability company, whether or not an agreement to pay that compensation was made before the services were rendered.
(s) Insure for its benefit the life of any of its members, managers, officers, or employees, insure the life of any member for the purpose of acquiring at his or her death the interest owned by the member, and continue the insurance after the relationship terminates.
(t) Carry out every other act not inconsistent with law that is appropriate to promote and attain the purposes set forth in its articles of organization.

(Added by Stats. 2012, Ch. 419, Sec. 20. Effective January 1, 2013. Operative January 1, 2014, by Sec. 32 of Ch. 419.)

17701.06.

The law of this state governs all of the following:
(a) The internal affairs of a limited liability company.
(b) The liability of a member as member and a manager as manager for the debts, obligations, or other liabilities of a limited liability company.
(c) The authority of the members and agents of a limited liability company.

(Added by Stats. 2012, Ch. 419, Sec. 20. Effective January 1, 2013. Operative January 1, 2014, by Sec. 32 of Ch. 419.)

17701.07.

(a) It is the policy of this title and this state to give maximum effect to the principles of freedom of contract and to the enforceability of operating agreements.
(b) Unless displaced by particular provisions of this title, the principles of law and equity supplement this title.

ARTICLE 1. General Provisions [17701.01 - 17701.17]

(c) Rules that statutes in derogation of the common law are to be strictly construed shall have no application to this title.
(d) Unless the context otherwise requires, as used in this title, the singular shall include the plural and the plural may refer to only the singular. The use of any gender shall be applicable to all genders.

(Added by Stats. 2012, Ch. 419, Sec. 20. Effective January 1, 2013. Operative January 1, 2014, by Sec. 32 of Ch. 419.)

17701.08.

(a) The name of a limited liability company shall contain the words "limited liability company," or the abbreviation "L.L.C." or "LLC." "Limited" may be abbreviated as "Ltd.," and "company" may be abbreviated as "Co."
(b) Unless authorized by subdivision (c), the name of a limited liability company shall not be a name that the Secretary of State determines is likely to mislead the public and shall be distinguishable in the records of the Secretary of State from all of the following:
   (1) The name of any limited liability company or foreign limited liability company authorized to transact business in this state.
   (2) Each name reserved under Section 17701.09.
(c) A limited liability company may apply to the Secretary of State for authorization to use a name that does not comply with subdivision (b). The Secretary of State shall authorize use of the name applied for if, as to each noncomplying name, either of the following applies:
   (1) The present user, registrant, or owner of the noncomplying name consents in a signed record to the use and submits an undertaking in a form satisfactory to the Secretary of State to change the noncomplying name to a name that complies with subdivision (b) and is distinguishable in the records of the Secretary of State from the name applied for.
   (2) The applicant delivers to the Secretary of State a certified copy of the final judgment of a court establishing the applicant's right to use in this state the name applied for.
(d) Subject to Section 17708.04, this section applies to a foreign limited liability company transacting intrastate business in this state that has a certificate of registration to transact intrastate business in this state or that has applied for a certificate of registration.
(e) The name shall not include the words "bank," "trust," "trustee," "incorporated," "inc.," "corporation," or "corp." and shall not include the words "insurer" or "insurance company" or any other words suggesting that it is in the business of issuing policies of insurance and assuming insurance risks.

(Added by Stats. 2012, Ch. 419, Sec. 20. Effective January 1, 2013. Operative January 1, 2014, by Sec. 32 of Ch. 419.)

17701.09.

(a) A person may reserve the exclusive use of the name of a limited liability company or foreign limited liability company, including an alternative name for a foreign limited liability company whose name is not available, by delivering an application to the Secretary of State. The application shall state the name and address of the applicant and the name proposed to be reserved. If the Secretary of State finds that the name applied for is available, it shall be reserved for the applicant's exclusive use for up to 60 days. The Secretary of State shall not issue certificates reserving the same name for two or more consecutive 60-day periods to the same applicant or for the use or benefit of the same person; nor shall consecutive reservations be made by or for the use or benefit of the same person for a name so similar as to fall within the prohibitions of subdivision (b) of Section 17701.08.
(b) The owner of a name reserved for a limited liability company or foreign limited liability company may transfer the reservation to another person by delivering to the Secretary of State for filing a signed notice of the transfer which states the name and address of the transferee.

(Added by Stats. 2012, Ch. 419, Sec. 20. Effective January 1, 2013. Operative January 1, 2014, by Sec. 32 of Ch. 419.)

17701.10.

(a) Except as otherwise provided in this section, the operating agreement governs all of the following:
   (1) Relations among the members as members and between the members and the limited liability company.
   (2) The rights and duties under this title of a person in the capacity of manager.
   (3) The activities of the limited liability company and the conduct of those activities.
   (4) The means and conditions for amending the operating agreement.
(b) To the extent the operating agreement does not otherwise provide for a matter described in subdivision (a), this title governs the matter.
(c) An operating agreement shall not do any of the following:
   (1) Vary a limited liability company's capacity under Section 17701.05 to sue and be sued in its own name.
   (2) Vary the law applicable under Section 17701.06.
   (3) Vary the power of the court under Section 17702.04.
   (4) Subject to subdivisions (d) to (g), inclusive, eliminate the duty of loyalty, the duty of care, or any other fiduciary duty.
   (5) Subject to subdivisions (d) to (g), inclusive, eliminate the contractual obligation of good faith and fair dealing under subdivision (d) of Section 17704.09.
   (6) Unreasonably restrict the duties and rights stated in Section 17704.10.
   (7) Vary the power of a court to decree dissolution in the circumstances specified in subdivision (a) of Section 17707.03 or the provisions for avoidance of dissolution in subdivision (c) of Section 17707.03.

ARTICLE 1. General Provisions [17701.01 - 17701.17]

(8) Except as stated herein, vary the requirements of Sections 17707.04 to 17707.08, inclusive.

(9) Unreasonably restrict the right of a member to maintain an action under Article 9 (commencing with Section 17709.01).

(10) Restrict the right to approve a merger, conversion, or domestication under Section 17710.14 to a member that will have personal liability with respect to a surviving, converted, or domesticated organization.

(11) Except as otherwise provided in subdivision (b) of Section 17701.12, restrict the rights under this title of a person other than a member or manager.

(12) Vary any provision under Article 10 (commencing with Section 17710.01).

(13) Vary any provision under Article 12 (commencing with Section 17712.01).

(14) Eliminate the duty of loyalty under subdivision (b) of Section 17704.09, but the operating agreement may do any of the following:
   (A) Identify specific types or categories of activities that do not violate the duty of loyalty, if not manifestly unreasonable.
   (B) Specify the number or percentage of members that may authorize or ratify, after full disclosure to all members of all material facts, a specific act or transaction that otherwise would violate the duty of loyalty.

(15) Unreasonably reduce the duty of care under subdivision (c) of Section 17704.09.

(16) Eliminate the obligation of good faith and fair dealing under subdivision (d) of Section 17704.09, but the operating agreement may prescribe the standards by which the performance of the obligation is to be measured, if the standards are not manifestly unreasonable.

(d) Except as provided in subdivision (c) and subdivisions (e) to (g), inclusive, the effects of the provisions of this title may be varied as among the members or as between the members and the limited liability company by the operating agreement; provided, however, that the provisions of Sections 17701.13, 17703.01, 17704.07, and 17704.08 shall only be varied by a written operating agreement. Notwithstanding the first sentence of this subdivision and in addition to the matters specified in subdivision (c), the operating agreement shall not do either of the following:
   (1) Vary the definitions of Section 17701.02, except as specifically provided therein.
   (2) Vary a member's rights under Sections 17703.01 and 17704.10.

(e) The fiduciary duties of a manager to the limited liability company and to the members of the limited liability company shall only be modified in a written operating agreement with the informed consent of the members. Assenting to the operating agreement pursuant to subdivision (b) of Section 17701.11 shall not constitute informed consent.

(f) To the extent the operating agreement of a member-managed limited liability company expressly relieves a member of a responsibility that the member would otherwise have under this title and imposes the responsibility on one or more other members, the operating agreement may, to the benefit of the member that the operating agreement relieves of the responsibility, also eliminate or limit any fiduciary duty that would have pertained to the responsibility.

(g) The operating agreement may alter or eliminate the indemnification for a member or manager provided by subdivision (a) of Section 17704.08 and may eliminate or limit a member or manager's liability to the limited liability company and members for money damages, except for the following:
   (1) Breach of the duty of loyalty.
   (2) A financial benefit received by the member or manager to which the member or manager is not entitled.
   (3) A member's liability for excess distributions under Section 17704.06.
   (4) Intentional infliction of harm on the limited liability company or a member.
   (5) An intentional violation of criminal law.

(Added by Stats. 2012, Ch. 419, Sec. 20. Effective January 1, 2013. Operative January 1, 2014, by Sec. 32 of Ch. 419.)

17701.11.

(a) A limited liability company is bound by and may enforce the operating agreement.
(b) A person that becomes a member of a limited liability company is deemed to assent to the operating agreement.
(c) Two or more persons intending to become the initial members of a limited liability company may make an agreement providing that upon the formation of the limited liability company the agreement will become the operating agreement. One person intending to become the initial member of a limited liability company may assent to terms providing that upon the formation of the limited liability company the terms will become the operating agreement.

(Added by Stats. 2012, Ch. 419, Sec. 20. Effective January 1, 2013. Operative January 1, 2014, by Sec. 32 of Ch. 419.)

17701.12.

(a) An operating agreement may specify that its amendment requires the approval of a person that is not a party to the operating agreement or the satisfaction of a condition. An amendment is ineffective if its adoption does not include the required approval or satisfy the specified condition.
(b) The obligations of a limited liability company and its members to a person in the person's capacity as a transferee or dissociated member are governed by the operating agreement. Subject only to any court order issued under paragraph (2) of subdivision (b) of Section 17705.03 to effectuate a charging order, an amendment to the operating agreement made after a person becomes a transferee or dissociated member is effective with regard to any debt, obligation, or other liability of the limited liability company or its members to the person in the person's capacity as a transferee or dissociated member.
(c) If a record that has been delivered by a limited liability company to the Secretary of State for filing and has become effective under this title contains a provision that

ARTICLE 1. General Provisions [17701.01 - 17701.17]

would be ineffective under subdivision (c) of Section 17701.10 if contained in the operating agreement, the provision is likewise ineffective in the record.
(d) Subject to subdivision (c), if a record that has been delivered by a limited liability company to the Secretary of State for filing and has become effective under this title conflicts with a provision of the operating agreement both of the following apply:
  (1) The operating agreement prevails as to members, dissociated members, transferees, and managers.
  (2) The record prevails as to other persons to the extent they reasonably rely on the record.

(Added by Stats. 2012, Ch. 419, Sec. 20. Effective January 1, 2013. Operative January 1, 2014, by Sec. 32 of Ch. 419.)

17701.13.

(a) A limited liability company shall designate and continuously maintain in this state both of the following:
  (1) An office, which need not be a place of its activity in this state.
  (2) An agent for service of process.
(b) A foreign limited liability company that has a certificate of registration under Section 17708.02 shall designate and continuously maintain in this state an agent for service of process.
(c) An agent for service of process of a limited liability company or foreign limited liability company shall be an individual who is a resident of this state or a corporation that has complied with Section 1505 and whose capacity to act as an agent has not terminated. If a limited liability company or foreign limited liability company designates a corporation as its agent for service of process in an instrument filed with the Secretary of State, no address for that agent for service of process shall be set forth in that instrument.
(d) Each limited liability company shall maintain in writing or in any other form capable of being converted into clearly legible tangible form at the office referred to in subdivision (a) all of the following:
  (1) A current list of the full name and last known business or residence address of each member and of each holder of a transferable interest in the limited liability company set forth in alphabetical order, together with the contribution and the share in profits and losses of each member and holder of a transferable interest.
  (2) If the limited liability company is a manager-managed limited liability company, a current list of the full name and business or residence address of each manager.
  (3) A copy of the articles of organization and all amendments thereto, together with any powers of attorney pursuant to which the articles of organization or any amendments thereto were executed.
  (4) Copies of the limited liability company's federal, state, and local income tax or information returns and reports, if any, for the six most recent fiscal years.
  (5) A copy of the limited liability company's operating agreement, if in writing, and any amendments thereto, together with any powers of attorney pursuant to

which any written operating agreement or any amendments thereto were executed.
(6) Copies of the financial statement of the limited liability company, if any, for the six most recent fiscal years.
(7) The books and records of the limited liability company as they relate to the internal affairs of the limited liability company for at least the current and past four fiscal years.

(e) Upon request of an assessor, a domestic or foreign limited liability company owning, claiming, possessing, or controlling property in this state subject to local assessment shall make available at the limited liability company's principal office in this state or at the office required to be kept pursuant to subdivision (a) or at a place mutually acceptable to the assessor and the limited liability company a true copy of the business records relevant to the amount, cost, and value of all property that the limited liability company owns, claims, possesses, or controls within the county.

(Added by Stats. 2012, Ch. 419, Sec. 20. Effective January 1, 2013. Operative January 1, 2014, by Sec. 32 of Ch. 419.)

17701.14.

(a) A limited liability company or foreign limited liability company may change its designated office, its principal office, its agent for service of process, the address of its agent for service of process, its mailing address, or, in the case of a foreign limited liability company, its principal business office in this state by delivering to the Secretary of State for filing a statement of information as set forth in Section 17702.09.
(b) A statement of information is effective when filed by the Secretary of State.

(Added by Stats. 2012, Ch. 419, Sec. 20. Effective January 1, 2013. Operative January 1, 2014, by Sec. 32 of Ch. 419.)

17701.15.

(a) To resign as an agent for service of process of a limited liability company or foreign limited liability company, the agent shall deliver to the Secretary of State for filing a signed and acknowledged statement of resignation containing the limited liability company name, the Secretary of State's file number, the name of resigning agent for service of process, and a statement that the agent is resigning.
(b) The Secretary of State shall file a statement of resignation delivered under subdivision (a) and mail or otherwise provide or deliver a copy to the designated office of the limited liability company or, in the case of a foreign limited liability company, to the principal office.
(c) Upon filing of the statement of resignation, the authority of the agent to act in that capacity shall cease.
(d) If an individual who has been designated agent for service of process dies or resigns or no longer resides in the state, or if the corporate agent for that purpose resigns,

ARTICLE 1. General Provisions [17701.01 - 17701.17]

dissolves, withdraws from the state, forfeits its right to transact intrastate business in this state, has its corporate rights, powers, and privileges suspended, or ceases to exist, the limited liability company or foreign limited liability company shall promptly file an initial or amended statement of information as set forth in Section 17702.09.

(Added by Stats. 2012, Ch. 419, Sec. 20. Effective January 1, 2013. Operative January 1, 2014, by Sec. 32 of Ch. 419.)

17701.16.

(a) In addition to Chapter 4 (commencing with Section 413.10) of Title 5 of Part 2 of the Code of Civil Procedure, process may be served upon limited liability companies and foreign limited liability companies as provided in this section.

(b) Personal service of a copy of any process against the limited liability company or the foreign limited liability company by delivery (1) to any individual designated by it as agent, or (2) if the designated agent is a corporation, to any person named in the latest certificate of the corporate agent filed pursuant to Section 1505 at the office of the corporate agent, shall constitute valid service on the limited liability company or the foreign limited liability company. No change in the address of the agent for service of process or appointment of a new agent for service of process shall be effective until an amendment to the statement described in Section 17701.14 is filed. In the case of a foreign limited liability company that has appointed the Secretary of State as agent for service of process pursuant to subdivision (d) of Section 17708.07, process shall be delivered by hand to the Secretary of State, or to any person employed in the capacity of assistant or deputy, and shall include one copy of the process for each defendant to be served, together with a copy of the court order authorizing the service and the fee therefor. The order shall set forth the address to which the process shall be sent by the Secretary of State.

(c) If an agent for service of process has resigned and has not been replaced or if the designated agent cannot with reasonable diligence be found at the address designated for personal delivery of the process, and it is shown by affidavit to the satisfaction of the court that process against a limited liability company or foreign limited liability company cannot be served with reasonable diligence upon the designated agent by hand in the manner provided in Section 415.10, subdivision (a) of Section 415.20, or subdivision (a) of Section 415.30 of the Code of Civil Procedure, the court may make an order that the service shall be made upon a domestic limited liability company or upon a registered foreign limited liability company by delivering by hand to the Secretary of State, or to any person employed in the Secretary of State's office in the capacity of assistant or deputy, one copy of the process for each defendant to be served, together with a copy of the order authorizing the service. Service in this manner shall be deemed complete on the 10th day after delivery of the process to the Secretary of State.

(d) Upon receipt of the copy of process and the fee therefor, the Secretary of State shall give notice of the service of the process to the limited liability company or foreign

limited liability company, at its principal office, by forwarding to that office, by registered mail with request for return receipt, the copy of the process.
(e) The Secretary of State shall keep a record of all process served upon the Secretary of State under this title and shall record therein the time of service and the action taken by the Secretary of State. A certificate under the Secretary of State's official seal, certifying to the receipt of process, the giving of notice to the limited liability company or foreign limited liability company, and the forwarding of the process pursuant to this section, shall be competent and prima facie evidence of the service of process.

(Added by Stats. 2012, Ch. 419, Sec. 20. Effective January 1, 2013. Operative January 1, 2014, by Sec. 32 of Ch. 419.)

17701.17.

(a) A member may, in a written operating agreement or other writing, consent to be subject to the nonexclusive jurisdiction of the courts of a specified jurisdiction and the courts of this state, or the exclusive jurisdiction of the courts of this state.
(b) If a member desires to use the arbitration process, that member may, in a written operating agreement or other writing, consent to be nonexclusively subject to arbitration in a specified state or states and this state, or to be exclusively subject to arbitration in this state.
(c) Along with this consent to the jurisdiction of courts or arbitration, a member may consent to be served with legal process in the manner prescribed in the operating agreement or other writing.

(Added by Stats. 2012, Ch. 419, Sec. 20. Effective January 1, 2013. Operative January 1, 2014, by Sec. 32 of Ch. 419.)

ARTICLE 2. Formation: Articles of Organization and Other Filings [17702.01 - 17702.10]

17702.01.

(a) One or more persons may act as organizers to form a limited liability company by signing and delivering to the Secretary of State for filing articles of organization on a form prescribed by the Secretary of State.
(b) The articles of organization shall state all of the following:
    (1) A statement that the purpose of the limited liability company is to engage in any lawful act or activity for which a limited liability company may be organized under this title.
    (2) The name of the limited liability company, which shall comply with Section 17701.08.
    (3) The street address of the initial designated office and the mailing address of the limited liability company if different from the street address of the initial designated office.

ARTICLE 2. Formation: Articles of Organization and Other Filings [17702.01 - 17702.10]

(4) The name and street address of the initial agent for service of process of the limited liability company who meets the qualifications specified in subdivision (c) of Section 17701.13. If a corporate agent is designated, only the name of the agent shall be set forth.

(5) If the limited liability company is to be manager-managed, the articles of organization shall contain a statement to that effect.

(6) If the limited liability company is to be managed by only one manager, the articles of organization shall contain a statement to that effect.

(c) Subject to subdivision (c) of Section 17701.12, articles of organization may also contain any other provision not inconsistent with law other than those provisions required by subdivision (b).

(d) A limited liability company is formed when the Secretary of State has filed the articles of organization.

(e) Except in a proceeding by this state to dissolve a limited liability company, the filing of the articles of organization by the Secretary of State is conclusive proof that the organizer satisfied all conditions to the formation of a limited liability company.

(f) The Secretary of State may cancel the filing of the articles of organization if a check or other remittance accepted in payment of the filing fee is not paid upon presentation. Upon receiving written notification that the item presented for payment has not been honored for payment, the Secretary of State shall give a first written notice of the applicability of this subdivision to the agent for service of process or to the person submitting the instrument. Thereafter, if the amount has not been paid by cashier's check or equivalent, the Secretary of State shall give a second written notice of cancellation and the cancellation shall thereupon be effective. The second notice shall be given 20 days or more after the first notice, and 90 days or less after the original filing.

(g) The Secretary of State shall include with the instructional materials, provided in conjunction with the form for filing the articles of organization under subdivision (a), a notice that filing the registration will obligate the limited liability company to pay an annual tax for that taxable year to the Franchise Tax Board pursuant to Section 17941 of the Revenue and Taxation Code. That notice shall be updated annually to specify the dollar amount of the tax.

(Added by Stats. 2012, Ch. 419, Sec. 20. Effective January 1, 2013. Operative January 1, 2014, by Sec. 32 of Ch. 419.)

17702.02.

(a) The articles of organization may be amended or restated at any time.

(b) To amend its articles of organization, a limited liability company shall deliver to the Secretary of State for filing a certificate of amendment, on a form prescribed by the Secretary of State, stating all of the following:

(1) The present name of the limited liability company.

(2) The Secretary of State's file number for the limited liability company.

(3) The changes the amendment makes to the articles of organization as most recently amended or restated.

(c) To restate its articles of organization, a limited liability company shall deliver to the Secretary of State for filing a restatement, on a form prescribed by the Secretary of State, stating, as applicable, the following:
   (1) The present name of the limited liability company and the Secretary of State's file number for the limited liability company.
   (2) The changes the restatement makes to the articles of organization as most recently amended or restated.
(d) Subject to subdivision (c) of Section 17701.12 and subdivision (c) of Section 17702.05, an amendment to or restatement of the articles of organization is effective when filed by the Secretary of State and shall be duly executed by at least one manager of a manager-managed limited liability company or at least one member of a member-managed limited liability company unless a greater number is provided in the articles of organization.
(e) If a member of a member-managed limited liability company, or a manager of a manager-managed limited liability company, knows that any information in filed articles of organization was inaccurate when the articles were filed or has become inaccurate owing to changed circumstances, the member or manager shall promptly do the following:
   (1) Cause the articles to be amended.
   (2) If appropriate, deliver to the Secretary of State for filing a statement of information under Section 17701.14 or a certificate of correction under Section 17702.06.
(f) A limited liability company shall not amend its articles of organization pursuant to subdivision (b) or restate its articles of organization pursuant to subdivision (c) in order to change its designated office, its mailing address, its agent for service of process, or the address of its agent for service of process. To change that information, the limited liability company shall deliver to the Secretary of State for filing a statement of information under Section 17701.14.

(Added by Stats. 2012, Ch. 419, Sec. 20. Effective January 1, 2013. Operative January 1, 2014, by Sec. 32 of Ch. 419.)

17702.03.

(a) A record delivered to the Secretary of State for filing pursuant to this title shall be signed as follows:
   (1) Except as otherwise provided in paragraphs (2) and (3), a record signed on behalf of a limited liability company shall be signed by a person authorized by the limited liability company.
   (2) A limited liability company's initial articles of organization shall be signed by at least one person acting as an organizer.
   (3) A record filed on behalf of a dissolved limited liability company that has no members shall be signed by the person winding up the limited liability company's activities or a person appointed under Section 17707.04 to wind up those activities.

ARTICLE 2. Formation: Articles of Organization and Other Filings [17702.01 - 17702.10]

    (4) A certificate of cancellation under Section 17707.02 shall be signed by each organizer that signed the initial articles of organization, but a personal representative of a deceased or incompetent organizer may sign in the place of the decedent or incompetent.

(b) Any record filed under this title may be signed by an agent.

(c) A limited liability company may record in the office of the county recorder of any county in this state, and county recorders, on request, shall record a certified copy of the limited liability company articles of organization and any exhibit or attachment, or any amendment or correction thereto, that has been filed in the office of the Secretary of State. A foreign limited liability company may record in the office of the county recorder of any county in the state a certified copy of the application for registration of the foreign limited liability company, or any amendment thereto, that has been filed in the office of the Secretary of State. The recording shall create a conclusive presumption in favor of any bona fide purchaser or encumbrancer for value of the limited liability company real property located in the county in which the certified copy has been recorded, of the statements contained therein.

(d) If the Secretary of State determines that an instrument submitted for filing or otherwise submitted does not conform to the law and returns it to the person submitting it, the instrument may be resubmitted accompanied by a written opinion of a member of the State Bar of California submitting the instrument or representing the person submitting it, to the effect that the specific provisions of the instrument objected to by the Secretary of State do conform to law and stating the points and authorities upon which the opinion is based. The Secretary of State shall rely, with respect to any disputed point of law, other than the application of Sections 17701.08, 17701.09, 17708.02, and 17708.03, upon that written opinion in determining whether the instrument conforms to law. The date of filing in that case shall be the date the instrument is received on resubmission.

(Added by Stats. 2012, Ch. 419, Sec. 20. Effective January 1, 2013. Operative January 1, 2014, by Sec. 32 of Ch. 419.)

17702.04.

(a) If a person required by this title to sign a record or deliver a record to the Secretary of State for filing under this title does not do so, any other person that is aggrieved may petition the superior court to order any of the following:
    (1) The person to sign the record.
    (2) The person to deliver the record to the Secretary of State for filing.
    (3) The Secretary of State to file the record unsigned.

(b) If a petitioner under subdivision (a) is not the limited liability company or foreign limited liability company to which the record pertains, the petitioner shall make the limited liability company a party to the action.

(Added by Stats. 2012, Ch. 419, Sec. 20. Effective January 1, 2013. Operative January 1, 2014, by Sec. 32 of Ch. 419.)

17702.05.

(a) A record authorized or required to be delivered to the Secretary of State for filing under this title shall be captioned to describe the record's purpose, be in a medium permitted by the Secretary of State, and be delivered to the Secretary of State. If the filing fees have been paid, unless the Secretary of State determines that a record does not comply with applicable laws, the Secretary of State shall file the record.

(b) Upon request and payment of the requisite fee, the Secretary of State shall send to the requester a certified copy of a requested record.

(c) Except for original articles of organization and except as otherwise provided in Sections 17701.14 and 17702.06, a record delivered to the Secretary of State for filing under this title may specify a delayed effective date. Subject to Section 17702.06, a record filed by the Secretary of State is effective as follows:
   (1) If the record does not specify a delayed effective date, on the date the record is filed as evidenced by the Secretary of State's endorsement of the date on the record.
   (2) If the record specifies a delayed effective date, on the date specified in the record. A delayed effective date specified in the record shall not be more than 90 days after the date the record is filed.

(d) In the case of a delayed effective date, the instrument may be prevented from becoming effective by a certificate stating that by appropriate action it has been revoked and is null and void. This certificate shall be executed in the same manner as the original instrument and shall be filed before the delayed effective date.

(e) In the case of a merger agreement or certificate of merger, a certificate revoking the earlier filing need only be executed on behalf of one of the constituent parties to the merger. If no revocation certificate is filed, the instrument becomes effective on the date specified.

(Added by Stats. 2012, Ch. 419, Sec. 20. Effective January 1, 2013. Operative January 1, 2014, by Sec. 32 of Ch. 419.)

17702.06.

(a) A limited liability company or foreign limited liability company may deliver to the Secretary of State for filing a certificate of correction on a form prescribed by the Secretary of State to correct a record previously delivered by the limited liability company or foreign limited liability company to the Secretary of State and filed by the Secretary of State, if at the time of filing the record contained inaccurate information or was defectively signed.

(b) A certificate of correction under subdivision (a) may not state a delayed effective date and shall do all of the following:
   (1) State the present name of the limited liability company or foreign limited liability company and the Secretary of State's file number.
   (2) Describe the title to the document to be corrected, including its filing date.
   (3) Set forth the name of each party to the document to be corrected.

ARTICLE 2. Formation: Articles of Organization and Other Filings [17702.01 - 17702.10]

    (4) Specify the inaccurate information and the reason it is inaccurate or the manner in which the signing was defective.

    (5) Correct the defective signature or inaccurate information.

(c) When filed by the Secretary of State, a certificate of correction under subdivision (a) is effective retroactively as of the effective date of the record the certificate corrects, but the statement is effective when filed as to persons that previously relied on the uncorrected record and would be adversely affected by the retroactive effect.

(Added by Stats. 2012, Ch. 419, Sec. 20. Effective January 1, 2013. Operative January 1, 2014, by Sec. 32 of Ch. 419.)

17702.07.

(a) If a record delivered to the Secretary of State for filing under this title and filed by the Secretary of State contains inaccurate information, a person that suffers a loss by reliance on the information may recover damages for the loss from the following:

    (1) A person that signed the record, or caused another to sign it on the person's behalf, and knew the information to be inaccurate at the time the record was signed.

    (2) Subject to subdivision (b), a member of a member-managed limited liability company or the manager of a manager-managed limited liability company, if all of the following apply:

        (A) The record was delivered for filing on behalf of the limited liability company.

        (B) The member or manager had notice of the inaccuracy for a reasonably sufficient time before the information was relied upon so that, before the reliance, the member or manager reasonably could have done all of the following:

            (i) Effected an amendment under Section 17702.02.

            (ii) Filed a petition under Section 17702.04.

            (iii) Delivered to the Secretary of State for filing a statement of information under Section 17701.14 or a certificate of correction under Section 17702.06.

(b) To the extent that the operating agreement of a member-managed limited liability company expressly relieves a member of responsibility for maintaining the accuracy of information contained in records delivered on behalf of the limited liability company to the Secretary of State for filing under this title and imposes that responsibility on one or more other members, the liability stated in paragraph (2) of subdivision (a) applies to those other members and not to the member that the operating agreement relieves of the responsibility.

(c) An individual who signs a record authorized or required to be filed under this title affirms under penalty of perjury that the information stated in the record is accurate.

(Added by Stats. 2012, Ch. 419, Sec. 20. Effective January 1, 2013. Operative January 1, 2014, by Sec. 32 of Ch. 419.)

17702.09.

(a) Every limited liability company and every foreign limited liability company registered to transact intrastate business in this state shall deliver to the Secretary of State for filing within 90 days after the filing of its original articles of organization or registering to transact intrastate business and biennially thereafter during the applicable filing period, on a form prescribed by the Secretary of State, a statement of information containing:
  (1) The name of the limited liability company and the Secretary of State's file number and, in the case of a foreign limited liability company, the name under which the foreign limited liability company is authorized to transact intrastate business in this state and the state or other jurisdiction under the laws of which it is organized.
  (2) The name and street address of the agent in this state for service of process required to be maintained pursuant to Section 17701.13. If a corporate agent is designated, only the name of the agent shall be set forth.
  (3) The street address of its principal office. In the case of a foreign limited liability company, the street address of its principal business office in this state, if any, and, in the case of a domestic limited liability company, the street address of the office required to be maintained pursuant to Section 17701.13.
  (4) The mailing address of the limited liability company or foreign limited liability company, if different from the street address of its principal office, or principal business office in this state, or, in the case of a domestic limited liability company, the street address of the office required to be maintained pursuant to Section 17701.13.
  (5) The name and complete business or residence addresses of any manager or managers and the chief executive officer, if any, appointed or elected in accordance with the articles of organization or operating agreement or, if no manager has been so elected or appointed, the name and business or residence address of each member.
  (6) If the limited liability company or foreign limited liability company chooses to receive renewal notices and any other notifications from the Secretary of State by electronic mail instead of by United States mail, the limited liability company or foreign limited liability company shall include a valid electronic mail address for the limited liability company or foreign limited liability company, or for the limited liability company's or foreign limited liability company's designee to receive those notices.
  (7) The general type of business that constitutes the principal business activity or the limited liability company or foreign limited liability company, such as, for example, manufacture of aircraft, wholesale liquor distributor, or retail department store.

(b) If there has been no change in the information contained in the last filed statement of information of the limited liability company or foreign limited liability company on file in the office of Secretary of State, the limited liability company or foreign limited liability company may, in lieu of filing the statement of information required by subdivision (a), advise the Secretary of State, on a form prescribed by the

ARTICLE 2. Formation: Articles of Organization and Other Filings [17702.01 - 17702.10]

Secretary of State, that no changes in the required information have occurred during the applicable filing period.

(c) For purposes of this section, the applicable filing period for a limited liability company shall be the calendar month during which its original articles of organization was filed or, in the case of a foreign limited liability company, the month during which its application for registration was filed, and the immediately preceding five calendar months. The Secretary of State shall provide a notice to each limited liability company or foreign limited liability company to comply with this section approximately three months prior to the close of the applicable filing period. The notice shall state the due date for compliance and shall be sent to the last mailing address of the limited liability company or foreign limited liability company according to the records of the Secretary of State, or if none, to the street address of the principal office, or, in the case of a domestic limited liability company, the office required to be maintained pursuant to Section 17701.13, or to the last electronic mail address according to the records of the Secretary of State if the limited liability company or foreign limited liability company has elected to receive notices from the Secretary of State by electronic mail. The failure of the limited liability company or foreign limited liability company to receive the notice shall not exempt the limited liability company or foreign limited liability company from complying with this section.

(d) Whenever any of the information required by subdivision (a) changes, other than the name and address of the agent for service of process, the limited liability company or foreign limited liability company may file a current statement containing all the information required by subdivision (a). When changing its agent for service of process or when the address of the agent changes, the limited liability company or foreign limited liability company shall file a current statement containing all the information required by subdivision (a). Whenever any statement is filed pursuant to this section, that statement supersedes any previously filed statement pursuant to this section, the statement in the original articles of organization, and the statement in any previously filed amended or restated articles of organization that have been filed, or in the case of a foreign limited liability company, in the application for registration.

(e) If a statement of information delivered to the Secretary of State for filing under this section does not contain the information required by subdivision (a), the Secretary of State shall promptly return the statement of information to the reporting limited liability company or foreign limited liability company for correction.

(f) The Secretary of State may destroy or otherwise dispose of any statement filed pursuant to this section after it has been superseded by the filing of a new statement.

(Added by Stats. 2012, Ch. 419, Sec. 20. Effective January 1, 2013. Operative January 1, 2014, by Sec. 32 of Ch. 419.)

17702.10.

An instrument shall be deemed filed, and the date of filing endorsed thereon, upon receipt by the Secretary of State of any instrument accompanied by the fee prescribed in Article 3 (commencing with Section 12180) of Chapter 3 of Part 2 of Division 3 of Title 2 of the

Government Code. The date of filing shall be the date the instrument is received by the Secretary of State unless the instrument provides that it is to be withheld from filing for a period of time not to exceed 90 days or unless, in the judgment of the Secretary of State, the filing is intended to be coordinated with the filing of some other document that cannot be filed. The Secretary of State shall file a document as of any requested future date not more than 90 days after its receipt, including a Saturday, Sunday, or legal holiday, if that document is received in the office of the Secretary of State at least one business day prior to the requested date of filing. Upon receipt and after filing of any document under this title, the Secretary of State may microfilm or reproduce by other techniques any filings or documents and destroy the original filing or document. The microfilm or other reproduction of any document under this section, or corresponding provision under prior law, shall be admissible in any court of law.

(Added by Stats. 2012, Ch. 419, Sec. 20. Effective January 1, 2013. Operative January 1, 2014, by Sec. 32 of Ch. 419.)

ARTICLE 3. Relations of Members and Managers to Persons Dealing with a Limited Liability Company [17703.01 - 17703.04]

17703.01.

(a) Unless the articles of organization indicate the limited liability company is a manager-managed limited liability company, every member is an agent of the limited liability company for the purpose of its business or affairs, and the act of any member, including, but not limited to, the execution in the name of the limited liability company of any instrument, for the apparent purpose of carrying on in the usual way the business or affairs of the limited liability company of which that person is a member, binds the limited liability company in the particular matter, unless the member so acting has, in fact, no authority to act for the limited liability company in the particular matter and the person with whom the member is dealing has actual knowledge of the fact that the member has no such authority.

(b) If the articles of organization indicate that the limited liability company is a manager-managed limited liability company, each of the following applies:

 (1) No member acting solely in the capacity of a member is an agent of the limited liability company nor can any member bind or execute any instrument on behalf of the limited liability company.

 (2) Every manager is an agent of the limited liability company for the purpose of its business or affairs, and the act of any manager, including, but not limited to, the execution in the name of the limited liability company of any instrument for apparently carrying on in the usual way the business or affairs of the limited liability company of which the person is a manager, binds the limited liability company, unless the manager so acting has, in fact, no authority to act for the limited liability company in the particular matter and the person with whom the manager is dealing has actual knowledge of the fact that the manager has no such authority.

ARTICLE 3. Relations of Members and Managers to Persons Dealing with a Limited Liability Company [17703.01 - 17703.04]

(c) No act of a manager or member in contravention of a restriction on authority shall bind the limited liability company to persons having actual knowledge of the restriction.
(d) Notwithstanding the provisions of subdivision (c), any note, mortgage, evidence of indebtedness, contract, certificate, statement, conveyance, or other instrument in writing, and any assignment or endorsement thereof, executed or entered into between any limited liability company and any other person, when signed by at least two managers, or by one manager in the case of a limited liability company whose articles of organization state that it is managed by only one manager, is not invalidated as to the limited liability company by any lack of authority of the signing managers or manager in the absence of actual knowledge on the part of the other person that the signing managers or manager had no authority to execute the same.

(Added by Stats. 2012, Ch. 419, Sec. 20. Effective January 1, 2013. Operative January 1, 2014, by Sec. 32 of Ch. 419.)

17703.04.

(a) All of the following apply to debts, obligations, or other liabilities of a limited liability company, whether arising in contract, tort, or otherwise:
    (1) They are solely the debts, obligations, or other liabilities of the limited liability company to which the debts, obligations, or other liabilities relate.
    (2) They do not become the debts, obligations, or other liabilities of a member or manager solely by reason of the member acting as a member or manager acting as a manager for the limited liability company.
(b) A member of a limited liability company shall be subject to liability under the common law governing alter ego liability, and shall also be personally liable under a judgment of a court or for any debt, obligation, or liability of the limited liability company, whether that liability or obligation arises in contract, tort, or otherwise, under the same or similar circumstances and to the same extent as a shareholder of a corporation may be personally liable for any debt, obligation, or liability of the corporation; except that the failure to hold meetings of members or managers or the failure to observe formalities pertaining to the calling or conduct of meetings shall not be considered a factor tending to establish that a member or the members have alter ego or personal liability for any debt, obligation, or liability of the limited liability company where the articles of organization or operating agreement do not expressly require the holding of meetings of members or managers.
(c) Nothing in this section shall be construed to affect the liability of a member of a limited liability company to third parties for the member's participation in tortious conduct, or pursuant to the terms of a written guarantee or other contractual obligation entered into by the member, other than an operating agreement.
(d) A limited liability company or foreign limited liability company shall carry insurance or provide an undertaking to the same extent and in the same amount as is required by any law, rule, or regulation of this state that would be applicable to the limited liability company or foreign limited liability company were it a corporation

organized and existing or duly qualified for the transaction of intrastate business under the General Corporation Law.
(e) Notwithstanding subdivision (a), a member of a limited liability company may agree to be obligated personally for any or all of the debts, obligations, and liabilities of the limited liability company as long as the agreement to be so obligated is set forth in the articles of organization or in a written operating agreement that specifically references this subdivision.

(Added by Stats. 2012, Ch. 419, Sec. 20. Effective January 1, 2013. Operative January 1, 2014, by Sec. 32 of Ch. 419.)

ARTICLE 4. Relations of Members to Each Other and to the Limited Liability Company [17704.01 - 17704.10]

17704.01.

(a) If a limited liability company is to have only one member upon formation, the person becomes a member as agreed by that person and the organizer of the limited liability company. That person and the organizer may be, but need not be, different persons. If different, the organizer acts on behalf of the initial member.
(b) If a limited liability company is to have more than one member upon formation, those persons become members as agreed by the persons before the formation of the limited liability company. The organizer acts on behalf of the persons in forming the limited liability company and may be, but need not be, one of the persons.
(c) After formation of a limited liability company, a person becomes a member as follows:
  (1) As provided in the operating agreement.
  (2) As the result of a transaction effective under Article 10 (commencing with Section 17710.01).
  (3) With the consent of all the members.
  (4) If, within 90 consecutive days after the limited liability company ceases to have any members, the last person to have been a member, or the legal representative of that person, designates a person to become a member, and the designated person consents to become a member.
(d) A person may become a member without acquiring a transferable interest and without making or being obligated to make a contribution to the limited liability company.

(Added by Stats. 2012, Ch. 419, Sec. 20. Effective January 1, 2013. Operative January 1, 2014, by Sec. 32 of Ch. 419.)

17704.02.

A contribution may consist of tangible or intangible property or other benefit to a limited liability company, including money, services performed, promissory notes, other agreements to contribute money or property, and contracts for services to be performed.

ARTICLE 4. Relations of Members to Each Other and to the Limited Liability Company [17704.01 - 17704.10]

(Added by Stats. 2012, Ch. 419, Sec. 20. Effective January 1, 2013. Operative January 1, 2014, by Sec. 32 of Ch. 419.)

17704.03.

(a) A person's obligation to make a contribution to a limited liability company is not excused by the person's death, disability, or other inability to perform personally. If a person does not make a required contribution, the person or the person's estate is obligated to contribute money equal to the value of the part of the contribution that has not been made, at the option of the limited liability company.
(b) The obligation of a member to make a contribution to a limited liability company may be compromised only by consent of all the members. A conditional obligation of a member to make a contribution to a limited liability company shall not be enforced unless the conditions of the obligation have been satisfied or waived as to or by that member. Conditional obligations include contributions payable upon a discretionary call of a limited liability company before the time the call occurs.
(c) A creditor of a limited liability company that extends credit or otherwise acts in reliance on an obligation described in subdivision (a) may enforce the obligation.
(d) Nothing in this section shall be construed to affect the rights of third-party creditors of the limited liability company to seek equitable remedies or any rights existing under the Uniform Fraudulent Transfer Act (Chapter 1 (commencing with Section 3439) of Title 2 of Part 2 of Division 4 of the Civil Code).

(Added by Stats. 2012, Ch. 419, Sec. 20. Effective January 1, 2013. Operative January 1, 2014, by Sec. 32 of Ch. 419.)

17704.04.

(a) Any distributions made by a limited liability company before its dissolution and winding up shall be among the members in accordance with the operating agreement. If the operating agreement does not otherwise provide, distributions shall be on the basis of the value, as stated in the required records when the limited liability company decides to make the distribution, of the contributions the limited liability company has received from each member, except to the extent necessary to comply with any transfer effective under Section 17705.02 and any charging order in effect under Section 17705.03.
(b) A person has a right to a distribution before the dissolution and winding up of a limited liability company only if the limited liability company decides to make an interim distribution. Unless the articles of organization or written operating agreement provides otherwise, a person's dissociation does not entitle the person to a distribution, and, beginning on the date of dissociation, the dissociated person shall have only the right of a transferee of a transferable interest with respect to that person's interest in the limited liability company, and then only with respect to distributions, if any, to which a transferee is entitled under the operating agreement. If the dissociation is in violation of the operating agreement, the limited liability

company shall have the right to offset any damages for the breach of the operating agreement from the amounts, if any, otherwise distributable to the dissociated person with respect to that person's interest in the limited liability company.
(c) A person does not have a right to demand or receive a distribution from a limited liability company in any form other than money. A limited liability company may distribute an asset in kind if each part of the asset is fungible with each other part and each person receives a percentage of the asset equal in value to the person's share of distributions.
(d) If a member or transferee becomes entitled to receive a distribution, the member or transferee has the status of, and is entitled to all remedies available to, a creditor of the limited liability company with respect to the distribution.

(Added by Stats. 2012, Ch. 419, Sec. 20. Effective January 1, 2013. Operative January 1, 2014, by Sec. 32 of Ch. 419.)

17704.05.

(a) A limited liability company shall not make a distribution if after the distribution either of the following applies:
    (1) The limited liability company would not be able to pay its debts as they become due in the ordinary course of the limited liability company's activities.
    (2) The limited liability company's total assets would be less than the sum of its total liabilities plus the amount that would be needed, if the limited liability company were to be dissolved, wound up, and terminated at the time of the distribution, to satisfy the preferential rights upon dissolution, winding up, and termination of members whose preferential rights are superior to those of persons receiving the distribution.
(b) A limited liability company may base a determination that a distribution is not prohibited under subdivision (a) on financial statements prepared on the basis of accounting practices and principles that are reasonable in the circumstances or on a fair valuation or other method that is reasonable under the circumstances.
(c) Except as otherwise provided in subdivision (f), the effect of a distribution under subdivision (a) is measured as follows:
    (1) In the case of a distribution by purchase, redemption, or other acquisition of a transferable interest in the limited liability company, as of the date money or other property is transferred or debt incurred by the limited liability company.
    (2) In all other cases, as of the date the distribution is authorized, if the payment occurs within 120 days after that date, or the payment is made, if the payment occurs more than 120 days after the distribution is authorized.
(d) A limited liability company's indebtedness to a member incurred by reason of a distribution made in accordance with this section is at parity with the limited liability company's indebtedness to its general, unsecured creditors.
(e) A limited liability company's indebtedness, including indebtedness issued in connection with or as part of a distribution, is not a liability for purposes of subdivision (a) if the terms of the indebtedness provide that payment of principal and

ARTICLE 4. *Relations of Members to Each Other and to the Limited Liability Company [17704.01 - 17704.10]*

interest are made only to the extent that a distribution could be made to members under this section.
(f) If indebtedness is issued as a distribution, each payment of principal or interest on the indebtedness is treated as a distribution, the effect of which is measured on the date the payment is made.
(g) In subdivision (f) of Section 17701.02, "distribution" does not include amounts constituting reasonable compensation for present or past services or reasonable payments made in the ordinary course of business under a bona fide retirement plan or other benefits program.

(Added by Stats. 2012, Ch. 419, Sec. 20. Effective January 1, 2013. Operative January 1, 2014, by Sec. 32 of Ch. 419.)

17704.06.

(a) Except as otherwise provided in subdivision (b), if a member of a member-managed limited liability company or manager of a manager-managed limited liability company consents to a distribution made in violation of Section 17704.05, the member or manager is personally liable to the limited liability company for the amount of the distribution that exceeds the amount that could have been distributed without the violation of Section 17704.05.
(b) To the extent the operating agreement of a member-managed limited liability company expressly relieves a member of the authority and responsibility to consent to distributions and imposes that authority and responsibility on one or more other members, the liability stated in subdivision (a) applies to the other members and not the member that the operating agreement relieves of authority and responsibility.
(c) A person that receives a distribution knowing that the distribution to that person was made in violation of Section 17704.05 is personally liable to the limited liability company but only to the extent that the distribution received by the person exceeded the amount that could have been properly paid under Section 17704.05.
(d) A person against which an action is commenced because the person is liable under subdivision (a) may do all of the following:
  (1) Implead any other person that is subject to liability under subdivision (a) and seek to compel contribution from the person.
  (2) Implead any person that received a distribution in violation of subdivision (c) and seek to compel contribution from the person in the amount the person received in violation of subdivision (c).
(e) An action under this section is barred if not commenced within four years after the distribution.

(Added by Stats. 2012, Ch. 419, Sec. 20. Effective January 1, 2013. Operative January 1, 2014, by Sec. 32 of Ch. 419.)

17704.07.

(a) A limited liability company is a member-managed limited liability company unless the articles of organization and the operating agreement do either of the following:
  (1) Expressly provide that:
    (A) The limited liability company is or will be "manager-managed."
    (B) The limited liability company is or will be "managed by managers."
    (C) Management of the limited liability company is or will be "vested in managers."
  (2) Include words of similar import.
(b) In a member-managed limited liability company, the following rules apply:
  (1) The management and conduct of the limited liability company are vested in the members.
  (2) Except as provided in subdivision (r), each member has equal rights in the management and conduct of the limited liability company's activities including equal voting rights.
  (3) A difference arising among members as to a matter in the ordinary course of the activities of the limited liability company shall be decided by a majority of the members of the limited liability company which the difference among the members has arisen.
  (4) An act outside the ordinary course of the activities of the limited liability company may be undertaken only with the consent of all members.
  (5) The operating agreement may be amended only with the consent of all members.
(c) In a manager-managed limited liability company, the following rules apply:
  (1) Except as otherwise expressly provided in this title, any matter relating to the activities of the limited liability company is decided exclusively by the managers.
  (2) Each manager has equal rights in the management and conduct of the activities of the limited liability company.
  (3) A difference arising among managers as to a matter in the ordinary course of the activities of the limited liability company may be decided by a majority of the managers of the limited liability company.
  (4) The consent of all members of the limited liability company is required to do any of the following:
    (A) Sell, lease, exchange, or otherwise dispose of all, or substantially all, of the limited liability company's property, with or without the goodwill, outside the ordinary course of the limited liability company's activities.
    (B) Approve a merger or conversion under Article 10 (commencing with Section 17710.01).
    (C) Undertake any other act outside the ordinary course of the limited liability company's activities.
    (D) Amend the operating agreement.
  (5) A manager may be chosen at any time by the consent of a majority of the members and remains a manager until a successor has been chosen, unless the manager at an earlier time resigns, is removed, or dies, or, in the case of a

ARTICLE 4. Relations of Members to Each Other and to the Limited Liability Company [17704.01 - 17704.10]

        manager that is not an individual, terminates. A manager may be removed at any time by the consent of a majority of the members without notice or cause.
      (6) A person need not be a member to be a manager, but the dissociation of a member that is also a manager removes the person as a manager. If a person that is both a manager and a member ceases to be a manager, that cessation does not by itself dissociate the person as a member.
      (7) A person's ceasing to be a manager does not discharge any debt, obligation, or other liability to the limited liability company or members which the person incurred while a manager.
(d) The dissolution of a limited liability company does not affect the applicability of this section. However, a person that wrongfully causes dissolution of the limited liability company loses the right to participate in management as a member and a manager.
(e) This title does not entitle a member to remuneration for services performed for a member-managed limited liability company, except for reasonable compensation for services rendered in winding up the activities of a limited liability company.
(f) Meetings of members may be held at any place, by electronic video screen communication or by electronic transmission by and to the limited liability company pursuant to paragraphs (1) and (2) of subdivision (i) of Section 17701.02, either within or without this state, selected by the person or persons calling the meeting or as may be stated in or fixed in accordance with the articles of organization or a written operating agreement. If no other place is stated or so fixed, all meetings shall be held at the principal office of the limited liability company. Unless prohibited by the articles of organization of the limited liability company, if authorized by the operating agreement, members not physically present in person or by proxy at a meeting of members may, by electronic transmission by and to the limited liability company pursuant to paragraphs (1) and (2) of subdivision (i) of Section 17701.02 or by electronic video screen communication, participate in a meeting of members, be deemed present in person or by proxy, and vote at a meeting of members whether that meeting is to be held at a designated place or in whole or in part by means of electronic transmission by and to the limited liability company or by electronic video screen communication, in accordance with subdivision (l).
(g) A meeting of the members may be called by any manager or by any member or members representing more than 10 percent of the interests in current profits of members for the purpose of addressing any matters on which the members may vote.
(h) (1) Whenever members are required or permitted to take any action at a meeting, a written notice of the meeting shall be given not less than 10 days nor more than 60 days before the date of the meeting to each member entitled to vote at the meeting. The notice shall state the place, date, and hour of the meeting, the means of electronic transmission by and to the limited liability company or electronic video screen communication, if any, and the general nature of the business to be transacted. No other business may be transacted at that meeting.
      (1) Any report or any notice of a members' meeting shall be given personally, by electronic transmission by the limited liability company, or by mail or other means of written communication, addressed to the member at the address of the member appearing on the books of the limited liability company or given by the

member to the limited liability company for the purpose of notice, or, if no address appears or is given, at the place where the principal office of the limited liability company is located or by publication at least once in a newspaper of general circulation in the county in which the principal office is located. The notice or report shall be deemed to have been given at the time when delivered personally, delivered by electronic transmission by the limited liability company, deposited in the mail, or sent by other means of written communication. An affidavit of mailing or delivered by electronic transmission by the limited liability company of any notice or report in accordance with this article, executed by a manager, shall be prima facie evidence of the giving of the notice or report.

(2) If any notice or report addressed to the member at the address of the member appearing on the books of the limited liability company is returned to the limited liability company by the United States Postal Service marked to indicate that the United States Postal Service is unable to deliver the notice or report to the member at the address, all future notices or reports shall be deemed to have been duly given without further mailing if they are available for the member at the principal office of the limited liability company for a period of one year from the date of the giving of the notice or report to all other members.

(3) Notice given by electronic transmission by the limited liability company under this subdivision shall be valid only if it complies with paragraph (1) of subdivision (i) of Section 17701.02.

(i) Notwithstanding this condition, notice shall not be given by electronic transmission by the limited liability company under this subdivision after either of the following has occurred:

(A) The limited liability company is unable to deliver two consecutive notices to the member by that means.

(B) The inability to so deliver the notices to the member becomes known to the secretary, any assistant secretary, the transfer agent, or any other person responsible for the giving of the notice.

(2) Upon written request to a manager by any person entitled to call a meeting of members, the manager shall immediately cause notice to be given to the members entitled to vote that a meeting will be held at a time requested by the person calling the meeting, not less than 10 days nor more than 60 days after the receipt of the request. If the notice is not given within 20 days after receipt of the request, the person entitled to call the meeting may give the notice or, upon the application of that person, the superior court of the county in which the principal office of the limited liability company is located, or if the principal office is not in this state, the county in which the limited liability company's address in this state is located, shall summarily order the giving of the notice, after notice to the limited liability company affording it an opportunity to be heard. The procedure provided in subdivision (c) of Section 305 shall apply to the application. The court may issue any order as may be appropriate, including, without limitation, an order designating the time and place of the meeting, the

ARTICLE 4. Relations of Members to Each Other and to the Limited Liability Company [17704.01 - 17704.10]

      record date for determination of members entitled to vote, and the form of notice.

        (i) When a members' meeting is adjourned to another time or place, unless the articles of organization or a written operating agreement otherwise require and except as provided in this subdivision, notice need not be given of the adjourned meeting if the time and place thereof or the means of electronic transmission by and to the limited liability company or electronic video screen communication, if any, are announced at the meeting at which the adjournment is taken. At the adjourned meeting, the limited liability company may transact any business that may have been transacted at the original meeting. If the adjournment is for more than 45 days, or if after the adjournment a new record date is fixed for the adjourned meeting, a notice of the adjourned meeting shall be given to each member of record entitled to vote at the meeting.

(j) The actions taken at any meeting of members, however called and noticed, and wherever held, have the same validity as if taken at a meeting duly held after regular call and notice, if a quorum is present either in person or by proxy, and if, either before or after the meeting, each of the members entitled to vote, not present in person or by proxy, provides a waiver of notice or consents to the holding of the meeting or approves the minutes of the meeting in writing. All waivers, consents, and approvals shall be filed with the limited liability company records or made a part of the minutes of the meeting after conversion to the form in which those records or minutes are kept. Attendance of a person at a meeting shall constitute a waiver of notice of the meeting, except when the person objects, at the beginning of the meeting, to the transaction of any business because the meeting is not lawfully called or convened. Attendance at a meeting is not a waiver of any right to object to the consideration of matters required by this title to be included in the notice but not so included, if the objection is expressly made at the meeting. Neither the business to be transacted nor the purpose of any meeting of members need be specified in any written waiver of notice, unless otherwise provided in the articles of organization or operating agreement, except as provided in subdivision (l).

(k) Members may participate in a meeting of the limited liability company through the use of conference telephones or electronic video screen communication, as long as all members participating in the meeting can hear one another, or by electronic transmission by and to the limited liability company pursuant to paragraphs (1) and (2) of subdivision (i) of Section 17701.02. Participation in a meeting pursuant to this provision constitutes presence in person at that meeting.

(l) Any action approved at a meeting, other than by unanimous approval of those entitled to vote, shall be valid only if the general nature of the proposal so approved was stated in the notice of meeting or in any written waiver of notice.

(m) (1) A majority of the members represented in person or by proxy shall constitute a quorum at a meeting of members.

    (1) The members present at a duly called or held meeting at which a quorum is present may continue to transact business until adjournment, notwithstanding the

loss of a quorum, if any action taken after loss of a quorum, other than adjournment, is approved by the requisite percentage of interests of members specified in this title or in the articles of organization or a written operating agreement.

(2) In the absence of a quorum, any meeting of members may be adjourned from time to time by the vote of a majority of the interests represented either in person or by proxy, but no other business may be transacted, except as provided in paragraph (2).

(n) (1) Any action that may be taken at any meeting of the members may be taken without a meeting if a consent in writing, setting forth the action so taken, is signed and delivered to the limited liability company within 60 days of the record date for that action by members having not less than the minimum number of votes that would be necessary to authorize or take that action at a meeting at which all members entitled to vote thereon were present and voted.

(1) Unless the consents of all members entitled to vote have been solicited in writing, (A) notice of any member approval of an amendment to the articles of organization or operating agreement, a dissolution of the limited liability company as provided in Section 17707.01, or a merger of the limited liability company as provided in Section 17710.10, without a meeting by less than unanimous written consent shall be given at least 10 days before the consummation of the action authorized by the approval, and (B) prompt notice shall be given of the taking of any other action approved by members without a meeting by less than unanimous written consent, to those members entitled to vote who have not consented in writing.

(2) Any member giving a written consent, or the member's proxyholder, may revoke the consent personally or by proxy by a writing received by the limited liability company prior to the time that written consents of members having the minimum number of votes that would be required to authorize the proposed action have been filed with the limited liability company, but may not do so thereafter. This revocation is effective upon its receipt at the office of the limited liability company required to be maintained pursuant to Section 17701.13.

(o) The use of proxies in connection with this section shall be governed in the same manner as in the case of corporations formed under the General Corporation Law, Division 1 (commencing with Section 100) of Title 1.

(p) In order that the limited liability company may determine the members of record entitled to notices of any meeting or to vote, or entitled to receive any distribution or to exercise any rights in respect of any other lawful action, a manager, or members representing more than 10 percent of the interests of members, may fix, in advance, a record date, that is not more than 60 days nor less than 10 days prior to the date of the meeting and not more than 60 days prior to any other action. If no record date is fixed the following shall apply:

(1) The record date for determining members entitled to notice of or to vote at a meeting of members shall be at the close of business on the business day next preceding the day on which notice is given or, if notice is waived, at the close of

ARTICLE 4. *Relations of Members to Each Other and to the Limited Liability Company [17704.01 - 17704.10]*

business on the business day next preceding the day on which the meeting is held.
  (2) The record date for determining members entitled to give consent to limited liability company action in writing without a meeting shall be the day on which the first written consent is given.
  (3) The record date for determining members for any other purpose shall be at the close of business on the day on which the managers adopt the resolution relating thereto, or the 60th day prior to the date of the other action, whichever is later.
  (4) The determination of members of record entitled to notice of or to vote at a meeting of members shall apply to any adjournment of the meeting unless a manager or the members who called the meeting fix a new record date for the adjourned meeting, but the manager or the members who called the meeting shall fix a new record date if the meeting is adjourned for more than 45 days from the date set for the original meeting.
(q) A meeting of the members may be conducted, in whole or in part, by electronic transmission by and to the limited liability company or by electronic video screen communication if both of the following requirements are met:
  (1) The limited liability company implements reasonable measures to provide members, in person or by proxy, a reasonable opportunity to participate in the meeting and to vote on matters submitted to the members, including an opportunity to read or hear the proceedings of the meeting substantially concurrently with those proceedings.
  (2) When any member votes or takes other action at the meeting by means of electronic transmission to the limited liability company or electronic video screen communication, a record of that vote or action shall be maintained by the limited liability company.
(r) The articles of organization or a written operating agreement may provide to all or certain identified members of a specified class or group of members the right to vote separately or with all or any class or group of members on any matter. Voting by members may be on a per capita, number, financial interest, class, group, or any other basis. If no voting provision is contained in the articles of organization or written operating agreement, each of the following shall apply:
  (1) The members of a limited liability company shall vote in proportion to their interests in current profits of the limited liability company or, in the case of a member who has assigned the member's entire transferable interest in the limited liability company to a person who has not been admitted as a member, in proportion to the interest in current profits that the assigning member would have, had the assignment not been made.
  (2) Any amendment to the articles of organization or operating agreement shall require the unanimous vote of all members.
  (3) In all other matters in which a vote is required, except as otherwise provided in this section, a vote of a majority of the members shall be sufficient.
(s) Notwithstanding any provision to the contrary in the articles of organization or operating agreement, in no event shall the articles of organization be amended by a vote of less than a majority of the members.

(t) Notwithstanding any provision to the contrary in the articles of organization or operating agreement, members shall have the right to vote on a dissolution of the limited liability company as provided in subdivision (b) of Section 17707.01 and on a merger of the limited liability company as provided in Section 17710.12.

(u) A written operating agreement may provide for the appointment of officers, including, but not limited to, a chairperson or a president, or both a chairperson and a president, a secretary, a chief financial officer, and any other officers with the titles, powers, and duties as shall be specified in the articles of organization or operating agreement or as determined by the managers or members. An officer may, but does not need to, be a member or manager of the limited liability company, and any number of offices may be held by the same person.

(v) Officers, if any, shall be appointed in accordance with the written operating agreement or, if no such provision is made in the operating agreement, any officers shall be appointed by the managers and shall serve at the pleasure of the managers, subject to the rights, if any, of an officer under any contract of employment. Any officer may resign at any time upon written notice to the limited liability company without prejudice to the rights, if any, of the limited liability under any contract to which the officer is a party.

(w) Subject to the provisions of the articles of organization, any note, mortgage, evidence of indebtedness, contract, certificate, statement, conveyance, or other instrument in writing, and any assignment or endorsement thereof, executed or entered into between any limited liability company and any other person, when signed by the chairperson of the board, the president, or any vice president and any secretary, any assistant secretary, the chief financial officer, or any assistant treasurer of the limited liability company, is not invalidated as to the limited liability company by any lack of authority of the signing officers in the absence of actual knowledge on the part of the other person that the signing officers had no authority to execute the same.

(Added by Stats. 2012, Ch. 419, Sec. 20. Effective January 1, 2013. Operative January 1, 2014, by Sec. 32 of Ch. 419.)

17704.08.

(a) A limited liability company shall reimburse for any payment made and indemnify for any debt, obligation, or other liability incurred by a member of a member-managed limited liability company or the manager of a manager-managed limited liability company in the course of the member's or manager's activities on behalf of the limited liability company, if, in making the payment or incurring the debt, obligation, or other liability, the member or manager complied with the duties stated in Section 17704.09.

(b) A limited liability company may purchase and maintain insurance on behalf of a member or manager of the limited liability company against liability asserted against or incurred by the member or manager in that capacity or arising from that status even if, under subdivision (g) of Section 17701.10, the operating agreement could not eliminate or limit the person's liability to the limited liability company for the conduct giving rise to the liability.

ARTICLE 4. Relations of Members to Each Other and to the Limited Liability Company [17704.01 - 17704.10]

(Added by Stats. 2012, Ch. 419, Sec. 20. Effective January 1, 2013. Operative January 1, 2014, by Sec. 32 of Ch. 419.)

17704.09.

(a) The fiduciary duties that a member owes to a member-managed limited liability company and the other members of the limited liability company are the duties of loyalty and care under subdivisions (b) and (c).
(b) A member's duty of loyalty to a limited liability company and the other members is limited to the following:
   (1) To account to a limited liability company and hold as trustee for it any property, profit, or benefit derived by the member in the conduct and winding up of the activities of a limited liability company or derived from a use by the member of a limited liability company property, including the appropriation of a limited liability company opportunity.
   (2) To refrain from dealing with a limited liability company in the conduct or winding up of the activities of a limited liability company as or on behalf of a party having an interest adverse to a limited liability company.
   (3) To refrain from competing with a limited liability company in the conduct or winding up of the activities of the limited liability company.
(c) A member's duty of care to a limited liability company and the other members in the conduct and winding up of the activities of the limited liability company is limited to refraining from engaging in grossly negligent or reckless conduct, intentional misconduct, or a knowing violation of law.
(d) A member shall discharge the duties to a limited liability company and the other members under this title or under the operating agreement and exercise any rights consistent with the obligation of good faith and fair dealing.
(e) A member does not violate a duty or obligation under this article or under the operating agreement merely because the member's conduct furthers the member's own interest.
(f) In a manager-managed limited liability company, all of the following rules apply:
   (1) Subdivisions (a), (b), (c), and (e) apply to the manager or managers and not the members.
   (2) Subdivision (d) applies to the members and managers.
   (3) Except as otherwise provided, a member does not have any fiduciary duty to the limited liability company or to any other member solely by reason of being a member.

(Added by Stats. 2012, Ch. 419, Sec. 20. Effective January 1, 2013. Operative January 1, 2014, by Sec. 32 of Ch. 419.)

17704.10.

(a) Upon the request of a member or holder of a transferable interest, for purposes reasonably related to the interest of that person as a member or a holder of a transferable interest, a manager or, if the limited liability company is member-managed, a member in possession of the requested information, shall promptly deliver, in writing, to the member or holder of a transferable interest, at the expense of the limited liability company, a copy of the information required to be maintained by paragraphs (1), (2), and (4) of subdivision (d) of Section 17701.13, and any written operating agreement of the limited liability company.

(b) Each member, manager, and holder of a transferable interest has the right, upon reasonable request, for purposes reasonably related to the interest of that person as a member, manager, or holder of a transferable interest, to each of the following:
  (1) To inspect and copy during normal business hours any of the records required to be maintained pursuant to Section 17701.13.
  (2) To obtain in writing from the limited liability company, promptly after becoming available, a copy of the limited liability company's federal, state, and local income tax returns for each year.

(c) In the case of a limited liability company with more than 35 members, each of the following shall apply:
  (1) A manager shall cause an annual report to be sent to each of the members not later than 120 days after the close of the fiscal year. The report, which may be sent by electronic transmission by the limited liability company (paragraph (1) of subdivision (i) of Section 17701.02) shall contain a balance sheet as of the end of the fiscal year and an income statement and a statement of cashflows for the fiscal year.
  (2) Members representing at least 5 percent of the voting interests of members, or three or more members, may make a written request to a manager for an income statement of the limited liability company for the initial three-month, six-month, or nine-month period of the current fiscal year ending more than 30 days prior to the date of the request, and a balance sheet of the limited liability company as of the end of that period. The statement shall be delivered or mailed to the members within 30 days thereafter.
  (3) The financial statements referred to in this section shall be accompanied by the report thereon, if any, of the independent accountants engaged by the limited liability company or, if there is no report, the certificate of the manager of the limited liability company that the financial statements were prepared without audit from the books and records of the limited liability company.

(d) A manager shall promptly furnish to a member a copy of any amendment to the articles of organization or operating agreement executed by a manager pursuant to a power of attorney from the member. The articles of organization or operating agreement may be sent by electronic transmission by the limited liability company.

(e) The limited liability company shall send or cause information to be sent in writing to each member or holder of a transferable interest within 90 days after the end of each taxable year the information necessary to complete federal and state income tax or information returns and, in the case of a limited liability company with 35 or fewer members, a copy of the limited liability company's federal, state, and local income tax or information returns for the year.

ARTICLE 5. Transferable Interests and Rights of Transferees and Creditors [17705.01 - 17705.04]

(f) In addition to the remedies provided in Sections 17713.06 and 17713.07 and any other remedies, a court of competent jurisdiction may enforce the duty of making and mailing or delivering the information and financial statements required by this section and, for good cause shown, extend the time therefor.

(g) In any action under this section or under Section 17713.07, if the court finds the failure of the limited liability company to comply with the requirements of this section is without justification, the court may award an amount sufficient to reimburse the person bringing the action for the reasonable expenses incurred by that person, including attorney's fees, in connection with the action or proceeding.

(h) Any waiver of the rights provided in this section shall be unenforceable.

(i) Any request, inspection, or copying by a member or holder of a transferable interest may be made by that person or by that person's agent or attorney.

(j) Upon complaint that a limited liability company is failing to comply with the provisions of this section, or to afford to the members rights given to them in the articles of organization or operating agreement, the Attorney General may, in the name of the people of the State of California, send to the office required to be maintained pursuant to Section 17701.13, notice of the complaint.

(k) If the answer of the limited liability company is not received within 30 days of the date the notice was transmitted, or if the answer is not satisfactory, and if the enforcement of the rights of the aggrieved persons by private civil action, by class action, or otherwise, would be so burdensome or expensive as to be impracticable, the Attorney General may institute, maintain, or intervene in any court of competent jurisdiction or before any administrative agency for relief by way of injunction, the dissolution of entities, the appointment of receivers, or any other temporary, preliminary, provisional, or final remedies as may be appropriate to protect the rights of members or to restore the position of the members for the failure to comply with the requirements of Section 17701.13 or the articles of organization or the operating agreement. In any action, suit, or proceeding, there may be joined as parties all persons and entities responsible for or affected by the activity.

(Added by Stats. 2012, Ch. 419, Sec. 20. Effective January 1, 2013. Operative January 1, 2014, by Sec. 32 of Ch. 419.)

ARTICLE 5. Transferable Interests and Rights of Transferees and Creditors [17705.01 - 17705.04]

17705.01.

A transferable interest is personal property.

(Added by Stats. 2012, Ch. 419, Sec. 20. Effective January 1, 2013. Operative January 1, 2014, by Sec. 32 of Ch. 419.)

17705.02.

(a) With respect to a transfer, in whole or in part, of a transferable interest, all of the following apply:
   (1) A transfer is permissible.
   (2) A transfer does not by itself cause a member's dissociation or a dissolution and winding up of the activities of a limited liability company.
   (3) Subject to Section 17705.04, a transfer does not entitle the transferee to do any of the following:
      (A) Participate in the management or conduct of the activities of a limited liability company.
      (B) Except as otherwise provided in subdivision (c), have access to records or other information concerning the activities of a limited liability company.
(b) A transferee has the right to receive, in accordance with the transfer, distributions to which the transferor would otherwise be entitled; provided, however, that the pledge or granting of a security interest, lien, or other encumbrance in or against any or all of the transferable interest of a transferor shall not cause the transferor to cease to be a member or grant to the transferee or to anyone else the power to exercise any rights or powers of a member, including, without limitation, the right to receive distributions to which the member is entitled.
(c) In a dissolution and winding up of a limited liability company, a transferee is entitled to an account of the limited liability company's transactions only from the date of dissolution.
(d) A transferable interest may be evidenced by a certificate of the interest issued by the limited liability company in a record, and, subject to this article, the interest represented by the certificate may be transferred by a transfer of the certificate.
(e) A limited liability company need not give effect to a transferee's rights under this section until the limited liability company has notice of the transfer.
(f) A transfer of a transferable interest in violation of a restriction on transfer contained in the operating agreement is ineffective as to a person having notice of the restriction at the time of transfer.
(g) Except as otherwise provided in subdivision (b) of this section and paragraph (2) of subdivision (d) of Section 17706.02, when a member transfers a transferable interest, the transferor retains the rights of a member, other than the interest in distributions transferred, and retains all duties and obligations of a member.
(h) When a member transfers a transferable interest to a person that becomes a member with respect to the transferred interest, the transferee is liable for the member's obligations under Section 17704.03 and subdivision (c) of Section 17704.06 known to the transferee when the transferee becomes a member.

(Added by Stats. 2012, Ch. 419, Sec. 20. Effective January 1, 2013. Operative January 1, 2014, by Sec. 32 of Ch. 419.)

ARTICLE 5. Transferable Interests and Rights of Transferees and Creditors [17705.01 - 17705.04]

17705.03.

(a) On application by a judgment creditor of a member or transferee, a court may enter a charging order against the transferable interest of the judgment debtor for the unsatisfied amount of the judgment. A charging order constitutes a lien on a judgment debtor's transferable interest and requires the limited liability company to pay over to the person to which the charging order was issued any distribution that would otherwise be paid to the judgment debtor.

(b) To the extent necessary to effectuate the collection of distributions pursuant to a charging order in effect under subdivision (a), the court may do any of the following:
  (1) Appoint a receiver of the distributions subject to the charging order, with the power to make all inquiries the judgment debtor might have made.
  (2) Make all other orders necessary to give effect to the charging order.
  (3) Upon a showing that distributions under a charging order will not pay the judgment debt within a reasonable time, foreclose the lien and order the sale of the transferable interest. The purchaser at the foreclosure sale obtains only the transferable interest, does not thereby become a member, and is subject to Section 17705.02.

(c) At any time before foreclosure under paragraph (3) of subdivision (b), the member or transferee whose transferable interest is subject to a charging order under subdivision (a) may extinguish the charging order by satisfying the judgment and filing a certified copy of the satisfaction with the court that issued the charging order.

(d) At any time before foreclosure under paragraph (3) of subdivision (b), a limited liability company or one or more members whose transferable interests are not subject to the charging order may pay to the judgment creditor the full amount due under the judgment and thereby succeed to the rights of the judgment creditor, including the charging order.

(e) This title does not deprive any member or transferee of the benefit of any exemption laws applicable to the member's or transferee's transferable interest.

(f) This section provides the exclusive remedy by which a person seeking to enforce a judgment against a member or transferee may, in the capacity of judgment creditor, satisfy the judgment from the judgment debtor's transferable interest.

(Added by Stats. 2012, Ch. 419, Sec. 20. Effective January 1, 2013. Operative January 1, 2014, by Sec. 32 of Ch. 419.)

17705.04.

If a member dies, the deceased member's personal representative or other legal representative may exercise the rights of a transferee provided in subdivision (c) of Section 17705.02 and, for the purposes of settling the estate, the rights of a current member under Section 17704.10.

(Added by Stats. 2012, Ch. 419, Sec. 20. Effective January 1, 2013. Operative January 1, 2014, by Sec. 32 of Ch. 419.)

California Revised Uniform Limited Liability Company Act

ARTICLE 6. Member's Dissociation [17706.01 - 17706.03]

17706.01.

(a) A person has the power to dissociate as a member at any time, rightfully or wrongfully, by withdrawing as a member by express will pursuant to subdivision (a) of Section 17706.02.
(b) A person's dissociation from a limited liability company is wrongful only if either of the following apply to the dissociation:
  (1) The dissociation is in breach of an express provision of the operating agreement.
  (2) The dissociation occurs before the termination of the limited liability company and any of the following:
    (A) The person withdraws as a member by express will.
    (B) The person is expelled as a member by judicial order under subdivision (e) of Section 17706.02.
    (C) The person is dissociated under subdivision (g) of Section 17706.02 by becoming a debtor in bankruptcy.
    (D) In the case of a person that is not a trust other than a business trust, an estate, or an individual, the person is expelled or otherwise dissociated as a member because it dissolved or terminated.
(c) A person that wrongfully dissociates as a member is liable to the limited liability company and to the other members for any damages caused by the dissociation. The liability is in addition to any other debt, obligation, or other liability of the member to the limited liability company or the other members.

(Added by Stats. 2012, Ch. 419, Sec. 20. Effective January 1, 2013. Operative January 1, 2014, by Sec. 32 of Ch. 419.)

17706.02.

A person is dissociated as a member from a limited liability company when any of the following occur:
(a) The limited liability company has notice of the person's express will to withdraw as a member, but, if the person specified a withdrawal date later than the date the limited liability company had notice, on that later date.
(b) An event stated in the operating agreement as causing the person's dissociation to occur.
(c) The person is expelled as a member pursuant to the operating agreement.
(d) The person is expelled as a member by the unanimous consent of the other members because any of the following applies:
  (1) It is unlawful to carry on the limited liability company's activities with the person as a member.
  (2) There has been a transfer of all of the person's transferable interest in the limited liability company, other than either of the following:
    (A) A transfer for security purposes.

ARTICLE 6. *Member's Dissociation [17706.01 - 17706.03]*

- (B) A charging order in effect under Section 17705.03 that has not been foreclosed.
- (3) The person is a corporation and, within 90 days after the limited liability company notifies the person that it will be expelled as a member because the person has filed a certificate of dissolution or the equivalent, its charter has been revoked, or its right to conduct business has been suspended by the jurisdiction of its incorporation and the certificate of dissolution has not been revoked or its charter or right to conduct business has not been reinstated.
- (4) The person is a limited liability company or partnership that has been dissolved and whose business is being wound up.
- (e) On application by the limited liability company, the person is expelled as a member by judicial order because the person has done any of the following:
  - (1) Engaged, or is engaging, in wrongful conduct that has adversely and materially affected, or will adversely and materially affect, the limited liability company's activities.
  - (2) Willfully or persistently committed, or is willfully and persistently committing, a material breach of the operating agreement or the person's duties or obligations under Section 17704.09.
  - (3) Engaged, or is engaging, in conduct relating to the limited liability company's activities that makes it not reasonably practicable to carry on the activities with the person as a member.
- (f) In the case of a person who is an individual, if either of the following applies:
  - (1) The person dies.
  - (2) In a member-managed limited liability company if either of the following applies:
    - (A) A guardian or general conservator for the person is appointed.
    - (B) There is a judicial order that the person has otherwise become incapable of performing the person's duties as a member under this title or the operating agreement.
- (g) In a member-managed limited liability company, the person becomes a debtor in bankruptcy.
- (h) In the case of a person that is a trust or is acting as a member by virtue of being a trustee of a trust, the trust's entire transferable interest in the limited liability company is distributed but not solely by reason of a substitution of a successor trustee.
- (i) In the case of a person that is an estate or is acting as a member by virtue of being a personal representative of an estate, the estate's entire transferable interest in the limited liability company is distributed but not solely by reason of a substitution of a successor personal representative.
- (j) In the case of a member that is not an individual, partnership, limited liability company, corporation, trust, or estate, the termination of the member.
- (k) The limited liability company participates in a merger under Article 10 (commencing with Section 17710.01), and either of the following applies:
  - (1) The limited liability company is not the surviving entity.
  - (2) Otherwise as a result of the merger, the person ceases to be a member.

(l) The limited liability company terminates.

(Added by Stats. 2012, Ch. 419, Sec. 20. Effective January 1, 2013. Operative January 1, 2014, by Sec. 32 of Ch. 419.)

17706.03.

(a) When a person is dissociated as a member of a limited liability company all of the following apply:
  (1) The person's right to participate as a member in the management and conduct of the limited liability company's activities terminates.
  (2) If the limited liability company is member-managed, the person's fiduciary duties as a member end with regard to matters arising and events occurring after the person's dissociation.
  (3) Subject to Section 17705.04 and Article 10 (commencing with Section 17710.01), any transferable interest owned by the person immediately before dissociation in the person's capacity as a member is owned by the person solely as a transferee.
(b) A person's dissociation as a member of a limited liability company does not of itself discharge the person from any debt, obligation, or other liability to the limited liability company or the other members that the person incurred while a member.

(Added by Stats. 2012, Ch. 419, Sec. 20. Effective January 1, 2013. Operative January 1, 2014, by Sec. 32 of Ch. 419.)

ARTICLE 7. Dissolution and Winding Up [17707.01 - 17707.09]

17707.01.

A limited liability company is dissolved, and its activities shall be wound up, upon the happening of the first to occur of the following:
(a) On the happening of an event set forth in a written operating agreement or the articles of organization.
(b) By the vote of a majority of the members of the limited liability company or a greater percentage of the voting interests of members as may be specified in the articles of organization, or a written operating agreement.
(c) The passage of 90 consecutive days during which the limited liability company has no members, except on the death of a natural person who is the sole member of a limited liability company, the status of the member, including a membership interest, may pass to the heirs, successors, and assigns of the member by will or applicable law. The heir, successor, or assign of the member's interest becomes a substituted member pursuant to subdivision (d) of Section 17704.01, subject to administration as provided by applicable law, without the permission or consent of the heirs, successors, or assigns or, those administering the estate of the deceased member.
(d) Entry of a decree of judicial dissolution pursuant to Section 17707.03.

ARTICLE 7. Dissolution and Winding Up [17707.01 - 17707.09]

(Added by Stats. 2012, Ch. 419, Sec. 20. Effective January 1, 2013. Operative January 1, 2014, by Sec. 32 of Ch. 419.)

17707.02.

(a) Notwithstanding any other provision of this title, if a domestic limited liability company has not conducted any business, only a majority of the members, or, if there are no members, the majority of the managers, if any, or if no members or managers, the person or a majority of the persons signing the articles of organization, may execute and acknowledge a certificate of cancellation of articles of organization, on a form prescribed by the Secretary of State, stating all of the following:
   (1) The name of the domestic limited liability company and the Secretary of State's file number.
   (2) That the certificate of cancellation is being filed within 12 months from the date the articles of organization was filed.
   (3) That the limited liability company does not have any debts or other liabilities, except as provided in paragraph (4).
   (4) That a final franchise tax return, as described by Section 23332 of the Revenue and Taxation Code, or a final annual tax return, as described by Section 17947 of the Revenue and Taxation Code, has been or will be filed with the Franchise Tax Board, as required under Part 10.2 (commencing with Section 18401) of Division 2 of the Revenue and Taxation Code.
   (5) That the known assets of the limited liability company remaining after payment of, or adequately providing for, known debts and liabilities have been distributed to the persons entitled thereto or that the limited liability company acquired no known assets, as the case may be.
   (6) That the limited liability company has not conducted any business from the time of the filing of the articles of organization.
   (7) That a majority of the managers or members voted, or, if no managers or members, the person or a majority of the persons signing the articles of organization, voted to dissolve the limited liability company.
   (8) If the limited liability company has received payments for interests from investors, that those payments have been returned to those investors.
(b) A certificate of cancellation executed and acknowledged pursuant to subdivision (a) shall be filed with the Secretary of State within 12 months from the date that the articles of organization was filed. The Secretary of State shall notify the Franchise Tax Board of the cancellation.
(c) Upon filing a certificate of cancellation pursuant to subdivision (a), a limited liability company shall be canceled and its powers, rights, and privileges shall cease.

(Added by Stats. 2012, Ch. 419, Sec. 20. Effective January 1, 2013. Operative January 1, 2014, by Sec. 32 of Ch. 419.)

California Revised Uniform Limited Liability Company Act

17707.03.

(a) Pursuant to an action filed by any manager or by any member or members of a limited liability company, a court of competent jurisdiction may decree the dissolution of a limited liability company whenever any of the events specified in subdivision (b) occurs.

(b) (1) It is not reasonably practicable to carry on the business in conformity with the articles of organization or operating agreement.

    (1) Dissolution is reasonably necessary for the protection of the rights or interests of the complaining members.

    (2) The business of the limited liability company has been abandoned.

    (3) The management of the limited liability company is deadlocked or subject to internal dissention.

    (4) Those in control of the limited liability company have been guilty of, or have knowingly countenanced persistent and pervasive fraud, mismanagement, or abuse of authority.

(c)

    (1) In any suit for judicial dissolution, the other members may avoid the dissolution of the limited liability company by purchasing for cash the membership interests owned by the members so initiating the proceeding, the "moving parties," at their fair market value. In fixing the value, the amount of any damages resulting if the initiation of the dissolution is a breach by any moving party or parties of an agreement with the purchasing party or parties, including, without limitation, the operating agreement, may be deducted from the amount payable to the moving party or parties; provided, that no member who sues for dissolution on the grounds set forth in paragraph (3), (4), or (5) of subdivision (a) shall be liable for damages for breach of contract in bringing that action.

    (2) If the purchasing parties elect to purchase the membership interests owned by the moving parties, are unable to agree with the moving parties upon the fair market value of the membership interests, and give bond with sufficient security to pay the estimated reasonable expenses, including attorney's fees, of the moving parties if the expenses are recoverable under paragraph (3), the court, upon application of the purchasing parties, either in the pending action or in a proceeding initiated in the superior court of the proper county by the purchasing parties, shall stay the winding up and dissolution proceeding and shall proceed to ascertain and fix the fair market value of the membership interests owned by the moving parties.

    (3) The court shall appoint three disinterested appraisers to appraise the fair market value of the membership interests owned by the moving parties, and shall make an order referring the matter to the appraisers so appointed for the purpose of ascertaining that value. The order shall prescribe the time and manner of producing evidence, if evidence is required. The award of the appraisers or a majority of them, when confirmed by the court, shall be final and conclusive upon all parties. The court shall enter a decree that shall provide in the alternative for winding up and dissolution of the limited liability company, unless payment is made for the membership interests within the time specified

ARTICLE 7. Dissolution and Winding Up [17707.01 - 17707.09]

by the decree. If the purchasing parties do not make payment for the membership interests within the time specified, judgment shall be entered against them and the surety or sureties on the bond for the amount of the expenses, including attorney's fees, of the moving parties. Any member aggrieved by the action of the court may appeal therefrom.
(4) If the purchasing parties desire to prevent the winding up and dissolution of the limited liability company, they shall pay to the moving parties the value of their membership interests ascertained and decreed within the time specified pursuant to this section, or, in the case of an appeal, as fixed on appeal. On receiving that payment or the tender of payment, the moving parties shall transfer their membership interests to the purchasing parties.
(5) For the purposes of this section, the valuation date shall be the date upon which the action for judicial dissolution was commenced. However, the court may, upon the hearing of a motion by any party, and for good cause shown, designate some other date as the valuation date.
(6) A dismissal of any suit for judicial dissolution by a manager, member, or members shall not affect the other members' rights to avoid dissolution pursuant to this section.

(Added by Stats. 2012, Ch. 419, Sec. 20. Effective January 1, 2013. Operative January 1, 2014, by Sec. 32 of Ch. 419.)

17707.04.

In the event of a dissolution of a limited liability company all of the following apply:
(a) The managers who have not wrongfully dissolved the limited liability company, or, if none, the members, or, if none, the person or a majority of the persons signing the articles of organization, may wind up the affairs of the limited liability company, unless the dissolution occurs pursuant to Section 17707.03, in which event the winding up shall be conducted in accordance with the decree of dissolution. The persons winding up the affairs of the limited liability company shall give written notice of the commencement of winding up by mail to all known creditors and claimants whose addresses appear on the records of the limited liability company.
(b) Upon the petition of any manager or of any member or members, or three or more creditors of a limited liability company, a court of competent jurisdiction may enter a decree ordering the winding up of the limited liability company, if that appears necessary for the protection of any parties in interest. The decree shall designate the managers or members, or if good cause is shown, another person or persons, who are to wind up the affairs of the limited liability company.
(c) Except as otherwise provided in the articles of organization or a written operating agreement, the persons winding up the affairs of the limited liability company pursuant to this section shall be entitled to reasonable compensation.

(Added by Stats. 2012, Ch. 419, Sec. 20. Effective January 1, 2013. Operative January 1, 2014, by Sec. 32 of Ch. 419.)

17707.05.

(a) Except as otherwise provided in the articles of organization or the written operating agreement, after determining that all the known debts and liabilities of a limited liability company in the process of winding up, including, without limitation, debts and liabilities to members who are creditors of the limited liability company, have been paid or adequately provided for, the remaining assets shall be distributed among the members according to their respective rights and preferences as follows:
   (1) To members in satisfaction of liabilities for distributions pursuant to Sections 17704.04, 17704.05, and 17704.06.
   (2) To members of the limited liability company for the return of their contributions.
   (3) To members in the proportions in which those members share in distributions.
(b) If the winding up is by court proceeding or subject to court supervision, the distribution shall not be made until after the expiration of any period for the presentation of claims that has been prescribed by order of the court.
(c) (1) The payment of a debt or liability, whether the whereabouts of the creditor is known or unknown, has been adequately provided for if the payment has been provided for by either of the following means:
   (A) Payment for the debt or liability has been assumed or guaranteed in good faith by one or more financially responsible persons or by the United States government or any agency of the United States government, and the provision, including the financial responsibility of the person, was determined in good faith and with reasonable care by the members or managers of the limited liability company to be adequate at the time of any distribution of the assets pursuant to this section.
   (B) The amount of the debt or liability has been deposited as provided in Section 2008 of the General Corporation Law.
   (2) This subdivision shall not prescribe the exclusive means of making adequate provision for debts and liabilities.

(Added by Stats. 2012, Ch. 419, Sec. 20. Effective January 1, 2013. Operative January 1, 2014, by Sec. 32 of Ch. 419.)

17707.06.

(a) A limited liability company that is dissolved nevertheless continues to exist for the purpose of winding up its affairs, prosecuting and defending actions by or against it in order to collect and discharge obligations, disposing of and conveying its property, and collecting and dividing its assets. A limited liability company shall not continue business except so far as necessary for its winding up.
(b) No action or proceeding to which a limited liability company is a party abates by the dissolution of the limited liability company or by reason of proceedings for its winding up and dissolution.

ARTICLE 7. Dissolution and Winding Up [17707.01 - 17707.09]

(c) Any assets inadvertently or otherwise omitted from the winding up continue in the dissolved limited liability company for the benefit of the persons entitled to those assets upon dissolution and on realization shall be distributed accordingly.

(d) After dissolution of the limited liability company, the limited liability company is bound by both of the following:

   (1) The act of a person authorized to wind up the affairs of the limited liability company, if the act is appropriate for winding up the activities of the limited liability company.

   (2) The act of a person authorized to act on behalf of the limited liability company, if the act would have bound the limited liability company before dissolution, if the other party to the transaction did not have notice of the dissolution.

(Added by Stats. 2012, Ch. 419, Sec. 20. Effective January 1, 2013. Operative January 1, 2014, by Sec. 32 of Ch. 419.)

17707.07.

(a)

   (1) Causes of action against a dissolved limited liability company, whether arising before or after the dissolution of the limited liability company, may be enforced against any of the following:

   (A) Against the dissolved limited liability company to the extent of its undistributed assets, including, without limitation, any insurance assets held by the limited liability company that may be available to satisfy claims.

   (B) If any of the assets of the dissolved limited liability company have been distributed to members, against members of the dissolved limited liability company to the extent of the limited liability company assets distributed to them upon dissolution of the limited liability company.

(b) Any member compelled to return distributed assets in an amount that exceeds the sum of the member's pro rata share of the claim and the amount for which the member could otherwise be held liable under Section 17704.05 or 17704.06 may seek contribution for the excess from any other member or manager, up to the sum of that other person's pro rata share of the claim and that other person's liabilities under Section 17704.05 or 17704.06.

   (1) Except as set forth in subdivision (c), all causes of action against a member of a dissolved limited liability company arising under this section are extinguished unless the claimant commences a proceeding to enforce the cause of action against that member of a dissolved limited liability company prior to the earlier of the following:

   (A) The expiration of the statute of limitations applicable to the cause of action.

   (B) Four years after the effective date of the dissolution of the limited liability company.

   (2) As a matter of procedure only, and not for purposes of determining liability, members of the dissolved limited liability company may be sued in the name of the limited liability company upon any cause of action against the limited liability company. This section does not affect the rights of the limited liability

company or its creditors under Sections 17704.05 and 17704.06, or the rights, if any, of creditors under the Uniform Fraudulent Transfer Act, that may arise against the member of a limited liability company.
(c) Summons or other process against a limited liability company may be served by delivering a copy thereof to a manager, member, officer, or person having charge of its assets or, if none of these persons can be found, to any agent upon whom process might be served at the time of dissolution. If none of those persons can be found with due diligence and it is so shown by affidavit to the satisfaction of the court, then the court may make an order that summons or other process be served upon the dissolved limited liability company by personally delivering a copy of the summons or other process, together with a copy of the order, to the Secretary of State or an assistant or Deputy Secretary of State. Service in this manner is deemed complete on the 10th day after delivery of the process to the Secretary of State. Upon receipt of process and the fee therefor, the Secretary of State shall give notice to the limited liability company as provided in Section 17701.16.
(d) Every limited liability company shall survive and continue to exist indefinitely for the purpose of being sued in any quiet title action. Any judgment rendered in that action shall bind each and all of its members or other persons having any equity or other interest in the limited liability company to the extent of that interest and the action shall have the same force and effect as an action brought under the provisions of Sections 410.50 and 410.60 of the Code of Civil Procedure. Service of summons or other process in any action may be made as provided in Chapter 4 (commencing with Section 413.10) of Title 5 of Part 2 of the Code of Civil Procedure or as provided in subdivision (b).
(e) For purposes of Article 4 (commencing with Section 19071) of Chapter 4 of Part 10.2 of Division 2 of the Revenue and Taxation Code, the liability described in this section shall be considered a liability at law with respect to a dissolved limited liability company.

(Added by Stats. 2012, Ch. 419, Sec. 20. Effective January 1, 2013. Operative January 1, 2014, by Sec. 32 of Ch. 419.)

17707.08.

(a)
  (1) The managers shall cause to be filed in the office of, and on a form prescribed by, the Secretary of State, a certificate of dissolution upon the dissolution of the limited liability company pursuant to Article 7 (commencing with Section 17707.01), unless the event causing the dissolution is that specified in subdivision (c) of Section 17707.01, in which case the persons conducting the winding up of the limited liability company's affairs pursuant to Section 17707.04 shall have the obligation to file the certificate of dissolution.
  (2) The certificate of dissolution shall set forth all of the following:
    (A) The name of the limited liability company and the Secretary of State's file number.

ARTICLE 7. *Dissolution and Winding Up [17707.01 - 17707.09]*

        (B) Any other information the persons filing the certificate of dissolution determine to include.
   (3) If a dissolution pursuant to subdivision (b) of Section 17707.01 is made by the vote of all of the members and a statement to that effect is added to the certificate of cancellation of articles of organization pursuant to subdivision (b), the separate filing of a certificate of dissolution pursuant to this subdivision is not required.
(b)
   (1) The persons who filed the certificate of dissolution shall cause to be filed in the office of, and on a form prescribed by, the Secretary of State, a certificate of cancellation of articles of organization upon the completion of the winding up of the affairs of the limited liability company pursuant to Section 17707.06, unless the event causing the dissolution is that specified in subdivision (c) of Section 17707.01, in that case the persons conducting the winding up of the limited liability company's affairs pursuant to Section 17707.04 shall have the obligation to file the certificate of cancellation of articles of organization.
   (2) The certificate of cancellation of articles of organization shall set forth all of the following:
        (A) The name of the limited liability company and the Secretary of State's file number.
        (B) That a final franchise tax return, as described by Section 23332 of the Revenue and Taxation Code, or a final annual tax return, as described by Section 17947 of the Revenue and Taxation Code, has been or will be filed with the Franchise Tax Board, as required under Part 10.2 (commencing with Section 18401) of Division 2 of the Revenue and Taxation Code.
        (C) Any other information the persons filing the certificate of cancellation of articles of organization determine to include.
   (3) The Secretary of State shall notify the Franchise Tax Board of the filing.
(c) Upon filing a certificate of cancellation pursuant to subdivision (b), a limited liability company shall be canceled and its powers, rights, and privileges shall cease.

(Added by Stats. 2012, Ch. 419, Sec. 20. Effective January 1, 2013. Operative January 1, 2014, by Sec. 32 of Ch. 419.)

17707.09.

(a) Notwithstanding the filing of a certificate of dissolution, a majority in interest of the members may cause to be filed, in the office of, and on a form prescribed by, the Secretary of State, a certificate of continuation, in any of the following circumstances:
   (1) The business of the limited liability company is to be continued pursuant to a unanimous vote of the remaining members.
   (2) The dissolution of the limited liability company was by vote of the members pursuant to subdivision (b) of Section 17707.01 and each member who consented to the dissolution has agreed in writing to revoke his or her vote in favor of or consent to the dissolution.

(3) The limited liability company was not, in fact, dissolved.
(b) The certificate of continuation shall set forth all of the following:
  (1) The name of the limited liability company and the Secretary of State's file number.
  (2) The grounds provided by subdivision (a) that are the basis for filing the certificate of continuation.
(c) Upon the filing of a certificate of continuation, the certificate of dissolution shall be of no effect from the time of the filing of the certificate of dissolution.

(Added by Stats. 2012, Ch. 419, Sec. 20. Effective January 1, 2013. Operative January 1, 2014, by Sec. 32 of Ch. 419.)

ARTICLE 8. Foreign Limited Liability Companies [17708.01 - 17708.09]

17708.01.

(a) The law of the state or other jurisdiction under which a foreign limited liability company is formed governs all of the following:
  (1) The organization of the limited liability company, its internal affairs, and the authority of its members and managers.
  (2) The liability of a member as member and a manager as manager for the debts, obligations, or other liabilities of the limited liability company.
(b) A foreign limited liability company shall not be denied a certificate of registration by reason of any difference between the law of the jurisdiction under which the limited liability company is formed and the law of this state.
(c) A certificate of registration does not authorize a foreign limited liability company to engage in any business or exercise any power that a limited liability company shall not engage in or exercise in this state.

(Added by Stats. 2012, Ch. 419, Sec. 20. Effective January 1, 2013. Operative January 1, 2014, by Sec. 32 of Ch. 419.)

17708.02.

(a) A foreign limited liability company may apply for a certificate of registration to transact business in this state by delivering an application to the Secretary of State for filing on a form prescribed by the Secretary of State. The application shall state all of the following:
  (1) The name of the foreign limited liability company, and, if the name does not comply with Section 17701.08, an alternate name adopted pursuant to subdivision (a) of Section 17708.05.
  (2) The state or other jurisdiction under whose law the foreign limited liability company is organized and the date of its organization in that state or other jurisdiction, and a statement that the foreign limited liability company is authorized to exercise its powers and privileges in that state or other jurisdiction.

ARTICLE 8. Foreign Limited Liability Companies [17708.01 - 17708.09]

(3) The street address of the foreign limited liability company's principal office and of its principal business office in this state, if any.

(4) The name and street address of the foreign limited liability company's initial agent for service of process in this state, who meets the qualifications specified in subdivision (c) of Section 17701.13. If a corporate agent is designated, only the name of the agent shall be set forth.

(5) A statement that the Secretary of State is appointed the agent of the foreign limited liability company for service of process if the agent has resigned and has not been replaced or if the agent cannot be found or served with the exercise of reasonable diligence.

(6) The mailing address of the foreign limited liability company if different than the street address of the principal office, or principal business office in this state.

(b) A foreign limited liability company shall deliver with a completed application under subdivision (a) a certificate of existence, status, or good standing or a record of similar import signed by the Secretary of State or other official having custody of the foreign limited liability company's publicly filed records in the state or other jurisdiction under whose law the foreign limited liability company is formed.

(c) The Secretary of State shall include with instructional materials, provided in conjunction with registration under subdivision (a), a notice that filing the registration will obligate the foreign limited liability company to pay an annual tax to the Franchise Tax Board pursuant to Section 17941 of the Revenue and Taxation Code. That notice shall be updated annually to specify the dollar amount of the tax.

(Added by Stats. 2012, Ch. 419, Sec. 20. Effective January 1, 2013. Operative January 1, 2014, by Sec. 32 of Ch. 419.)

17708.03.

(a) A foreign limited liability company that enters into repeated and successive transactions of business in this state, other than in interstate or foreign commerce, is considered to be transacting intrastate business in this state within the meaning of this article.

(b) Without excluding other activities that may not be considered to be transacting intrastate business in this state within the meaning of this article, activities of a foreign limited liability company that do not constitute transacting intrastate business in this state include all of the following:

(1) Maintaining or defending any action or suit or any administrative or arbitration proceeding, or effecting the settlement of those, or the settlement of claims or disputes.

(2) Carrying on any activity concerning its internal affairs, including holding meetings of its members or managers.

(3) Maintaining accounts in financial institutions.

(4) Maintaining offices or agencies for the transfer, exchange, and registration of the limited liability company's own securities or maintaining trustees or depositories with respect to those securities.

(5) Selling through independent contractors.

(6) Soliciting or procuring orders, whether by mail or electronic means or through employees or agents or otherwise, if the orders require acceptance outside this state before they become contracts.
(7) Creating or acquiring indebtedness, evidences of indebtedness, mortgages, liens, or security interests in real or personal property.
(8) Securing or collecting debts or enforcing mortgages or other security interests in property securing the debts and holding, protecting, or maintaining property so acquired.
(9) Conducting an isolated transaction that is completed within 180 days and is not in the course of a number of repeated transactions of a like nature.
(10) Transacting business in interstate commerce.
(c) Without excluding other activities that may not be considered to be transacting intrastate business in this state within the meaning of this article, a foreign limited liability company shall not be considered to be transacting intrastate business in this state merely because its subsidiary transacts intrastate business in this state, or merely because of its status as any one or more of the following:
(1) A shareholder of a domestic corporation.
(2) A shareholder of a foreign corporation transacting intrastate business.
(3) A limited partner of a foreign limited partnership transacting intrastate business.
(4) A limited partner of a domestic limited partnership.
(5) A member or manager of a foreign limited liability company transacting intrastate business.
(6) A member or manager of a domestic limited liability company.
(d) A person shall not be deemed to be transacting intrastate business in this state within the meaning of this article merely because of its status as a member or manager of a domestic limited liability company or a foreign limited liability company registered to transact intrastate business in this state.
(e) This section does not apply in determining the contacts or activities that may subject a foreign limited liability company to service of process, taxation, or regulation under the law of this state other than this article.

(Added by Stats. 2012, Ch. 419, Sec. 20. Effective January 1, 2013. Operative January 1, 2014, by Sec. 32 of Ch. 419.)

17708.04.

Unless the Secretary of State determines that an application for a certificate of registration does not comply with the filing requirements of this article, the Secretary of State, upon payment of all required filing fees, shall file the application of a foreign limited liability company, and issue a certificate of registration to transact intrastate business in this state to the foreign limited liability company or its representative.

(Added by Stats. 2012, Ch. 419, Sec. 20. Effective January 1, 2013. Operative January 1, 2014, by Sec. 32 of Ch. 419.)

ARTICLE 8. Foreign Limited Liability Companies [17708.01 - 17708.09]

17708.05.

(a) A foreign limited liability company whose name does not comply with Section 17701.08 shall not obtain a certificate of registration until it adopts, for the purpose of transacting intrastate business in this state, an alternate name that complies with Section 17701.08. A foreign limited liability company that adopts an alternate name under this subdivision and obtains a certificate of registration with the alternate name need not comply with fictitious or assumed name statutes. After obtaining a certificate of registration with an alternate name, a foreign limited liability company shall transact intrastate business in this state under the alternate name unless the limited liability company is authorized under fictitious or assumed name statutes to transact intrastate business in this state under another name.

(b) (1) If a foreign limited liability company authorized to transact intrastate business in this state changes its name or its alternate name adopted pursuant to subdivision (a), the foreign limited liability company shall not thereafter transact intrastate business in this state under that name or alternate name until it delivers an amended application to register, on a form prescribed by the Secretary of State, to the Secretary of State for filing.

    (A) If the new name of the foreign limited liability company does not comply with Section 17701.08, an alternate name shall be adopted pursuant to subdivision (a).

    (B) If the new name of the foreign limited liability company complies with Section 17701.08, the foreign limited liability company may not adopt an alternate name pursuant to subdivision (a).

    (C) If the foreign limited liability company is changing its alternate name, the new alternate name shall comply with Section 17701.08.

(2) The amended application for registration shall state the Secretary of State's file number, the name or alternate name relinquished, or the new name or new alternate name adopted under subdivision (a), or both.

(3) The foreign limited liability company shall deliver with the amended application to register a certificate, issued by the Secretary of State or other official having custody of the foreign limited liability company's publicly filed records in the state or other jurisdiction under whose law the limited liability company is formed, that certifies the change of name was made in accordance with the laws of that state or other jurisdiction. The certificate is not required if the foreign limited liability company is changing its alternate name adopted pursuant to subdivision (a).

(4) Upon the filing of the amended application to register with the Secretary of State, the Secretary of State shall issue to the foreign limited liability company a new certificate of registration in accordance with Section 17708.04.

(Added by Stats. 2012, Ch. 419, Sec. 20. Effective January 1, 2013. Operative January 1, 2014, by Sec. 32 of Ch. 419.)

17708.06.

(a) To cancel its certificate of registration to transact intrastate business in this state, a foreign limited liability company shall deliver to the Secretary of State for filing a certificate of cancellation stating the name under which the foreign limited liability company is authorized to transact intrastate business in this state, and the Secretary of State's file number. The certificate of registration is canceled when the notice becomes effective.

(b) The Secretary of State may cancel the application and certificate of registration of a foreign limited liability company if a check or other remittance accepted in payment of the filing fee is not paid upon presentation. Upon receiving written notification that the item presented for payment has not been honored for payment, the Secretary of State shall give a first written notice of the applicability of the section to the agent for service of process or to the person submitting the instrument. Thereafter, if the amount has not been paid by cashier's check or equivalent, the Secretary of State shall give a second written notice of cancellation and the cancellation shall thereupon be effective. The second notice shall be given 20 days or more after the first notice, and 90 days or less after the original filing.

(Added by Stats. 2012, Ch. 419, Sec. 20. Effective January 1, 2013. Operative January 1, 2014, by Sec. 32 of Ch. 419.)

17708.07.

(a) A foreign limited liability company transacting intrastate business in this state shall not maintain an action or proceeding in this state unless it has a certificate of registration to transact intrastate business in this state.

(b) The failure of a foreign limited liability company to have a certificate of registration to transact intrastate business in this state does not impair the validity of a contract or act of the foreign limited liability company or prevent the foreign limited liability company from defending an action or proceeding in this state.

(c) A member or manager of a foreign limited liability company is not liable for the debts, obligations, or other liabilities of the foreign limited liability company solely because the foreign limited liability company transacted intrastate business in this state without a certificate of registration.

(d) If a foreign limited liability company transacts intrastate business in this state without a certificate of registration or cancels its certificate of registration, it shall be deemed to have appointed the Secretary of State as its agent for service of process for rights of action arising out of the transaction of intrastate business in this state.

(Added by Stats. 2012, Ch. 419, Sec. 20. Effective January 1, 2013. Operative January 1, 2014, by Sec. 32 of Ch. 419.)

17708.08.

If the members of a foreign limited liability company residing in this state represent 25 percent or more of the voting interests of the members of that foreign limited liability company, those members shall be entitled to all information and inspection rights provided in Section 17704.10.

(Added by Stats. 2012, Ch. 419, Sec. 20. Effective January 1, 2013. Operative January 1, 2014, by Sec. 32 of Ch. 419.)

17708.09.

The Attorney General may maintain an action to enjoin a foreign limited liability company from transacting intrastate business in this state in violation of this title.

(Added by Stats. 2012, Ch. 419, Sec. 20. Effective January 1, 2013. Operative January 1, 2014, by Sec. 32 of Ch. 419.)

ARTICLE 9. Actions by Members [17709.01 - 17709.02]

17709.01.

Any member of a foreign or domestic limited liability company may bring a class action on behalf of all or a class of members to enforce any claim common to those members and any of those actions shall be governed by the law governing class actions generally, provided that in order to maintain the class action there shall be no requirement that the class be so numerous that joinder of all members of the class is impracticable.

(Added by Stats. 2012, Ch. 419, Sec. 20. Effective January 1, 2013. Operative January 1, 2014, by Sec. 32 of Ch. 419.)

17709.02.

(a) No action shall be instituted or maintained in right of any domestic or foreign limited liability company by any member of the limited liability company unless both of the following conditions exist:
    (1) The plaintiff alleges in the complaint that the plaintiff was a member of record, or beneficiary, at the time of the transaction or any part of the transaction of which the plaintiff complains, or that the plaintiff's interest later devolved upon the plaintiff by operation of law from a member who was a member at the time of the transaction or any part of the transaction complained of. Any member who does not meet these requirements may nevertheless be allowed in the discretion of the court to maintain the action on a preliminary showing to and determination by the court, by motion and after a hearing at which the court shall consider any evidence, by affidavit or testimony, as it deems material, of all of the following:
        (A) There is a strong prima facie case in favor of the claim asserted on behalf of the limited liability company.
        (B) No other similar action has been or is likely to be instituted.
        (C) The plaintiff acquired the interest before there was disclosure to the public or to the plaintiff of the wrongdoing of which plaintiff complains.

(D) Unless the action can be maintained, the defendant may retain a gain derived from defendant's willful breach of a fiduciary duty.

(E) The requested relief will not result in unjust enrichment of the limited liability company or any member of the limited liability company.

(2) The plaintiff alleges in the complaint with particularity the plaintiff's efforts to secure from the managers the action the plaintiff desires or the reasons for not making that effort, and alleges further that the plaintiff has either informed the limited liability company or the managers in writing of the ultimate facts of each cause of action against each defendant or delivered to the limited liability company or the managers a true copy of the complaint that the plaintiff proposes to file.

(b) In any action referred to in subdivision (a), at any time within 30 days after service of summons upon the limited liability company or upon any defendant who is a manager of the limited liability company or held that position at the time of the acts complained of, the limited liability company or the defendant may move the court for an order, upon notice and hearing, requiring the plaintiff to furnish security as hereinafter provided. The motion shall be based upon one or both of the following grounds:

(1) That there is no reasonable possibility that the prosecution of the cause of action alleged in the complaint against the moving party will benefit the limited liability company or its members.

(2) That the moving party, if other than the limited liability company did not participate in the transaction complained of in any capacity. The court, on application of the limited liability company or any defendant, may, for good cause shown, extend the 30-day period for an additional period not exceeding 60 days.

(c)

(1) At the hearing upon any motion pursuant to subdivision (b), the court shall consider evidence, written or oral, by witnesses or affidavit, as may be material to the ground upon which the motion is based, or to a determination of the probable reasonable expenses, including attorney's fees, of the limited liability company and the moving party that will be incurred in the defense of the action.

(2) If the court determines, after hearing the evidence adduced by the parties, that the moving party has established a probability in support of any of the grounds upon which the motion is based, the court shall fix the nature and amount of security, not to exceed fifty thousand dollars ($50,000), to be furnished by the plaintiff for reasonable expenses, including attorney's fees, that may be incurred by the moving party and the limited liability company in connection with the action. A ruling by the court on the motion shall not be a determination of any issue in the action or of the merits of the action. The amount of the security may thereafter be increased or decreased in the discretion of the court upon a showing that the security provided has or may become inadequate or is excessive, but the court shall not in any event increase the total amount of the security beyond fifty thousand dollars ($50,000) in the aggregate for all defendants. If the court, upon a motion, makes a determination that security

shall be furnished by the plaintiff as to any one or more defendants, the action shall be dismissed as to that defendant or those defendants, unless the security required by the court has been furnished within any reasonable time as shall be fixed by the court. The limited liability company and the moving party shall have recourse to the security in the amount that the court determines upon the termination of the action.

(d) If the plaintiff, either before or after a motion is made pursuant to subdivision (b), or any order or determination pursuant to that motion, posts good and sufficient bond or bonds in the aggregate amount of fifty thousand dollars ($50,000) to secure the reasonable expenses of the parties entitled to make the motion, the plaintiff shall be deemed to have complied with the requirements of this section and with any order for security made pursuant to this section. Any motion then pending shall be dismissed and no further or additional bond or other security shall be required.

(e) If a motion is filed pursuant to subdivision (b), no pleadings need be filed by the limited liability company or any other defendant and the prosecution of the action shall be stayed until 10 days after the motion has been disposed of.

(Added by Stats. 2012, Ch. 419, Sec. 20. Effective January 1, 2013. Operative January 1, 2014, by Sec. 32 of Ch. 419.)

ARTICLE 10. Merger and Conversion [17710.01 - 17710.19]

17710.01.

For purposes of this article, the following definitions apply:

(a) "Converted entity" means the other business entity or foreign other business entity or foreign limited liability company that results from a conversion of a domestic limited liability company under this title.

(b) "Converted limited liability company" means a domestic limited liability company that results from a conversion of an other business entity or a foreign other business entity or a foreign limited liability company pursuant to Section 17710.08.

(c) "Converting limited liability company" means a domestic limited liability company that converts to an other business entity or a foreign other business entity or a foreign limited liability company pursuant to this title.

(d) "Converting entity" means an other business entity or a foreign other business entity or a foreign limited liability company that converts to a domestic limited liability company pursuant to Section 17710.08.

(e) "Constituent corporation" means a corporation that is merged with or into one or more limited liability companies, foreign limited liability companies, or other business entities and that includes a surviving corporation.

(f) "Constituent limited liability company" means a limited liability company that is merged with or into one or more other limited liability companies, foreign limited liability companies, or other business entities and that includes a surviving limited liability company.

(g) "Constituent other business entity" means an other business entity that is merged with or into one or more limited liability companies or foreign limited liability companies and that includes a surviving other business entity.
(h) "Disappearing limited liability company" means a constituent limited liability company or foreign limited liability company that is not the surviving limited liability company.
(i) "Disappearing other business entity" means a constituent other business entity that is not the surviving other business entity.
(j) "Foreign other business entity" means an other business entity formed under the laws of a jurisdiction other than this state.
(k) "Other business entity" means a corporation, general partnership, limited partnership, business trust, real estate investment trust, or unincorporated association, other than a nonprofit association, but excludes a limited liability company or a foreign limited liability company.
(l) "Surviving limited liability company" means a limited liability company or foreign limited liability company into which one or more other limited liability companies, foreign limited liability companies, other business entities, or foreign business entities are merged.
(m) "Surviving other business entity" means an other business entity into which one or more limited liability companies or foreign limited liability companies are merged.

(Added by Stats. 2012, Ch. 419, Sec. 20. Effective January 1, 2013. Operative January 1, 2014, by Sec. 32 of Ch. 419.)

17710.02.

(a) A limited liability company may be converted into an other business entity or a foreign other business entity or a foreign limited liability company pursuant to this article if both of the following apply:
  (1) Pursuant to a conversion into a domestic or foreign general partnership or limited partnership or into a foreign limited liability company, each of the members of the converting limited liability company receives a percentage interest in the profits and capital of the converted entity equal to that member's percentage interest in profits and capital of the converting limited liability company as of the effective time of the conversion.
  (2) Pursuant to a conversion into an other business entity or foreign other business entity not specified in paragraph (1), both of the following occur:
    (A) Each limited liability company interest of the same class is treated equally with respect to any distribution of cash, property, rights, interests, or securities of the converted entity, unless all members of the class consent.
    (B) The nonredeemable limited liability company interests of the converting limited liability company are converted only into nonredeemable interests or securities of the converted entity, unless all holders of the unredeemable interests consent.

ARTICLE 10. *Merger and Conversion [17710.01 - 17710.19]*

(b) The conversion of a limited liability company to an other business entity or a foreign other business entity or a foreign limited liability company may be effected only if both of the following conditions are satisfied:
  (1) The law under which the converted entity will exist expressly permits the formation of that entity pursuant to a conversion.
  (2) The limited liability company complies with all other requirements of any other law that applies to conversion to the converted entity.

(Added by Stats. 2012, Ch. 419, Sec. 20. Effective January 1, 2013. Operative January 1, 2014, by Sec. 32 of Ch. 419.)

17710.03.

(a) A limited liability company that desires to convert to an other business entity or a foreign other business entity or a foreign limited liability company shall approve a plan of conversion.
The plan of conversion shall state all of the following:
  (1) The terms and conditions of the conversion.
  (2) The place of the organization of the converted entity and of the converting limited liability company and the name of the converted entity after conversion.
  (3) The manner of converting the membership interests of each of the members into shares of, securities of, or interests in, the converted entity.
  (4) The provisions of the governing documents for the converted entity, including the limited liability company articles of organization and operating agreement, or articles or certificate of incorporation if the converted entity is a corporation, to which the holders of interests in the converted entity are to be bound.
  (5) Any other details or provisions that are required by the laws under which the converted entity is organized, or that are desired by the parties.

(b)
  (1) The plan of conversion shall be approved by all managers and a majority in interest of each class of membership interest or if there are no managers, a majority in interest of each class of membership of the converting limited liability company, unless a greater or lesser approval is required by the operating agreement of the converting limited liability company.
  (2) However, if the members of the limited liability company would become personally liable for any obligations of the converted entity as a result of the conversion, the plan of conversion shall be approved by all of the limited members of the converting limited liability company, unless the plan of conversion provides that all members will have dissenters' rights as provided in Article 11 (commencing with Section 17711.01).

(c) Upon the effectiveness of the conversion, all members of the converting limited liability company, except those that exercise dissenters' rights as provided in Article 11 (commencing with Section 17711.01), shall be deemed parties to any governing documents for the converted entity adopted as part of the plan of conversion, regardless of whether or not the member has executed the plan of conversion or the governing documents for the converted entity. Any adoption of governing documents

made pursuant to the conversion shall be effective at the effective time or date of the conversion.
(d) Notwithstanding its prior approval, a plan of conversion may be amended before the conversion takes effect if the amendment is approved by all managers and a majority of the members or if there are no managers, a majority of the members of the converting limited liability company and, if the amendment changes any of the principal terms of the plan of conversion, the amendment is approved by the managers and members of the converting limited liability company in the same manner and to the same extent as required for the approval of the original plan of conversion.
(e) The managers by unanimous approval and the members of a converting limited liability company may, by majority approval at any time before the conversion is effective, in their discretion, abandon a conversion, without further approval by the managers or members, subject to the contractual rights of third parties other than managers or members.
(f) The converted entity shall keep the plan of conversion at the principal place of business of the converted entity if the converted entity is a domestic limited liability company or foreign other business entity, at the principal office of, or registrar or transfer agent of, the converted entity, if the converted entity is a domestic corporation, or at the office where records are to be kept pursuant to Section 17701.13 if the converted entity is a domestic limited liability company. Upon the request of a member of a converting limited liability company, the authorized person on behalf of the converted entity shall promptly deliver to the member or the holder of shares, interests, or other securities, at the expense of the converted entity, a copy of the plan of conversion. A waiver by a member of the rights provided in this subdivision shall be unenforceable.

(Added by Stats. 2012, Ch. 419, Sec. 20. Effective January 1, 2013. Operative January 1, 2014, by Sec. 32 of Ch. 419.)

17710.04.

(a) A conversion into an other business entity or a foreign other business entity or a foreign limited liability company shall become effective upon the earliest date that all of the following occur:
   (1) The plan of conversion is approved by the members of the converting limited liability company, as provided in Section 17710.03.
   (2) All documents required by law to create the converted entity are filed, which documents shall also contain a statement of conversion, if required under Section 17710.06.
   (3) The effective date, if set forth in the plan of conversion, occurs.
(b) A copy of the certificate of limited partnership, statement of partnership authority, articles of incorporation, or certificate of conversion complying with Section 17710.06, if applicable, duly certified by the Secretary of State, is conclusive evidence of the conversion of the limited liability company.

ARTICLE 10. Merger and Conversion [17710.01 - 17710.19]

(Added by Stats. 2012, Ch. 419, Sec. 20. Effective January 1, 2013. Operative January 1, 2014, by Sec. 32 of Ch. 419.)

17710.05.

(a) If the limited liability company is converting into a foreign limited liability company or foreign other business entity, those conversion proceedings shall be in accordance with the laws of the state or place of organization of the foreign limited liability company or foreign other business entity and the conversion shall become effective in accordance with that law.

(b)
   (1) To enforce an obligation of a limited liability company that has converted to a foreign limited liability company or foreign other business entity, the Secretary of State shall only be the agent for service of process in an action or proceeding against that converted foreign entity, if the agent designated for the service of process for that entity is a natural person and cannot be found with due diligence or if the agent is a corporation and no person, to whom delivery may be made, may be located with due diligence, or if no agent has been designated and if none of the officers, members, managers, or agents of that entity may be located after diligent search, and it is shown by affidavit to the satisfaction of the court. The court then may make an order that service be made by personal delivery to the Secretary of State or to an assistant or Deputy Secretary of State of two copies of the process together with two copies of the order, and the order shall set forth an address to which the process shall be sent by the Secretary of State. Service in this manner is deemed complete on the 10th day after delivery of the process to the Secretary of State.
   (2) Upon receipt of the process and order and the fee set forth in Section 12197 of the Government Code, the Secretary of State shall provide notice to that entity of the service of the process by forwarding by certified mail, return receipt requested, a copy of the process and order to the address specified in the order.
   (3) The Secretary of State shall keep a record of all process served upon the Secretary of State and shall record the time of service and the Secretary of State's action with respect to the process served. The certificate of the Secretary of State, under the Secretary of State's official seal, certifying to the receipt of process, the providing of notice of process to that entity, and the forwarding of the process shall be competent and prima facie evidence of the matters stated therein.

(Added by Stats. 2012, Ch. 419, Sec. 20. Effective January 1, 2013. Operative January 1, 2014, by Sec. 32 of Ch. 419.)

17710.06.

(a) Upon conversion of a limited liability company, one of the following applies:

(1) If the limited liability company is converting into a domestic limited partnership, a statement of conversion shall be completed on a certificate of limited partnership for the converted entity and shall be filed with the Secretary of State.

(2) If the limited liability company is converting into a domestic partnership, a statement of conversion shall be completed on the statement of partnership authority for the converted entity. If no statement of partnership authority is filed, a certificate of conversion shall be filed separately with the Secretary of State.

(3) If the limited liability company is converting into a domestic corporation, a statement of conversion shall be completed on the articles of incorporation for the converted entity and shall be filed with the Secretary of State.

(4) If the limited liability company is converting to a foreign limited liability company or foreign other business entity, a certificate of conversion shall be filed with the Secretary of State.

(b) Any certificate or statement of conversion shall be executed and acknowledged by all members, unless a lesser number is provided in the articles of organization or operating agreement, and shall set forth all of the following:

(1) The name and the Secretary of State's file number of the converting limited liability company.

(2) A statement that the principal terms of the plan of conversion were approved by a vote of the members, that equaled or exceeded the vote required under Section 17710.03, specifying each class entitled to vote and the percentage vote required of each class.

(3) The name, form and jurisdiction of organization, and Secretary of State's file number, if any, of the converted entity.

(4) The mailing address of the converted entity's agent for service of process and the chief executive office of the converted entity.

(c) The filing with the Secretary of State of a certificate of conversion, a certificate of limited partnership, a statement of partnership authority, or articles of incorporation containing a statement of conversion as set forth in subdivision (a) shall have the effect of the filing of a certificate of cancellation by the converting limited liability company, and no converting limited liability company that has made the filing is required to take any action under Article 7 (commencing with Section 17707.01) as a result of that conversion.

(d) For the purposes of this title, the certificate of conversion shall be on a form prescribed by the Secretary of State.

(Added by Stats. 2012, Ch. 419, Sec. 20. Effective January 1, 2013. Operative January 1, 2014, by Sec. 32 of Ch. 419.)

17710.07.

(a) Whenever a limited liability company or other business entity having any real property in this state converts into a limited liability company or an other business entity pursuant to the laws of this state or of the state or place where the limited liability company or other business entity was organized, and the laws of the state or place of organization, including this state, of the converting limited liability company or other converting entity provide substantially that the conversion vests in the converted limited liability company or other converted entity all the real property of the converting limited liability company or other converting entity, the filing for record in the office of the county recorder of any county in this state where any of the real property of the converting limited liability company or other converting entity is located of either of the following shall evidence record ownership in the converted limited liability company or other converted entity of all interest of the converting limited liability company or other converting entity in and to the real property located in that county:

(1) A certificate of conversion or a statement of partnership authority, a certificate of limited partnership, or articles of incorporation complying with Section 17710.06 certified on or after the effective date of the conversion by the Secretary of State.

(2) A copy of a certificate of conversion or a statement of partnership authority, certificate of limited partnership, articles of organization, articles of incorporation, or other certificate or document evidencing the creation of a foreign other business entity or foreign limited liability company by conversion, containing a statement of conversion, certified by the Secretary of State or an authorized public official of the state or place pursuant to the laws of which the conversion is effected.

(b) A filed and, if appropriate, recorded certificate of conversion or a statement of partnership authority, certificate of limited partnership, articles of organization, articles or certificate of incorporation, or other certificate evidencing the creation of a foreign other business entity or foreign limited liability company by conversion, containing a statement of conversion, filed pursuant to subdivision (a) of Section 17710.06, stating the name of the converting limited liability company or other converting entity in whose name property was held before the conversion and the name of the converted entity or converted limited liability company, but not containing all of the other information required by Section 17710.06, operates with respect to the entities named to the extent provided in subdivision (a).

(c) Recording of a certificate of conversion, or a statement of partnership authority, certificate of limited partnership, articles of organization, articles of incorporation, or other certificate evidencing the creation of an other business entity or a limited liability company by conversion, containing a statement of conversion, in accordance with subdivision (a), shall create, in favor of bona fide purchasers or encumbrances for value, a conclusive presumption that the conversion was validly completed.

(Added by Stats. 2012, Ch. 419, Sec. 20. Effective January 1, 2013. Operative January 1, 2014, by Sec. 32 of Ch. 419.)

17710.08.

(a) An other business entity or a foreign other business entity or a foreign limited liability company may be converted to a domestic limited liability company pursuant to this article only if the converting entity is authorized by the laws pursuant to which it is organized to effect the conversion.

(b) An other business entity or a foreign other business entity or a foreign limited liability company that desires to convert into a domestic limited liability company shall approve a plan of conversion or another instrument as is required to be approved to effect the conversion pursuant to the laws under which that entity is organized.

(c) The conversion of an other business entity or a foreign other business entity or a foreign limited liability company into a domestic limited liability company shall be approved by the number or percentage of the members, managers, shareholders, or holders of interest of the converting entity as is required by the laws under which that entity is organized, or a greater or lesser percentage, subject to applicable laws, as set forth in the converting entity's partnership agreement, articles of organization, operating agreement, articles or certificate of incorporation, or other governing document.

(d) The conversion by an other business entity or a foreign other business entity or a foreign limited liability company into a domestic limited liability company shall be effective under this article at the time the conversion is effective under the laws under which the converting entity is organized, as long as the articles of organization containing a statement of conversion has been filed with the Secretary of State. If the converting entity's governing law is silent as to the effectiveness of the conversion, the conversion shall be effective upon the completion of all acts required under this title to form a limited liability company.

(e) If the converting foreign limited liability company or foreign limited liability partnership is authorized to transact intrastate business in this state, the filing with the Secretary of State of its articles of organization containing a statement of conversion pursuant to the laws under which the converting foreign limited liability company or foreign other business entity is organized shall have the effect of the filing of a certificate of cancellation by the converting foreign limited partnership or foreign limited liability company and no converting foreign limited liability company or foreign limited partnership that has made the filing is required to file a certificate of cancellation under Section 15909.07 or 17708.06 as a result of that conversion. If a converting other business entity is a foreign corporation qualified to transact intrastate business in this state, the foreign corporation shall, by virtue of the filing, automatically surrender its right to transact intrastate business.

(Added by Stats. 2012, Ch. 419, Sec. 20. Effective January 1, 2013. Operative January 1, 2014, by Sec. 32 of Ch. 419.)

17710.09.

(a) An entity that converts into another entity pursuant to this article is for all purposes other than for the purposes of Part 10 (commencing with Section 17001), Part 10.2 (commencing with Section 18401), and Part 11 (commencing with Section 23001) of Division 2 of the Revenue and Taxation Code, the same entity that existed before the conversion and the conversion shall not be deemed a transfer of property.

ARTICLE 10. Merger and Conversion [17710.01 - 17710.19]

(b) Upon a conversion taking effect, all of the following apply:
   (1) All the rights and property, whether real, personal, or mixed, of the converting entity or converting limited liability company are vested in the converted entity or converted limited liability company.
   (2) All debts, liabilities, and obligations of the converting entity or converting limited liability company continue as debts, liabilities, and obligations of the converted entity or converted limited liability company.
   (3) All rights of creditors and liens upon the property of the converting entity or converting limited liability company shall be preserved unimpaired and remain enforceable against the converted entity or converted limited liability company to the same extent as against the converting entity or converting limited liability company as if the conversion had not occurred.
   (4) Any action or proceeding pending by or against the converting entity or converting limited liability company may be continued against the converted entity or converted limited liability company as if the conversion had not occurred.
(c) A member of a converting limited liability company is liable for both of the following:
   (1) All obligations of the converting limited liability company for which the member was personally liable before the conversion.
   (2) All obligations of the converted entity incurred after the conversion takes effect, but those obligations may be satisfied only out of property of the entity if that member of a limited liability company, or a shareholder in a corporation, or unless expressly provided otherwise in the articles of organization or other governing documents, a limited partner of a limited partnership, or a holder of equity securities in another converted entity if the holders of equity securities in that entity are not personally liable for the obligations of that entity under the law under which the entity is organized or its governing documents.
(d) A member of a converted limited liability company remains liable for any and all obligations of the converting entity for which the member was personally liable before the conversion, but only to the extent that the member was liable for the obligations of the converting entity prior to the conversion.
(e) If the other party to a transaction with the limited liability company reasonably believes when entering into the transaction that the limited liability company member is a general partner, the limited liability company member is liable for the obligations incurred by the limited liability company within 90 days after the conversion takes effect. The limited liability company member's liability for all other obligations of the limited liability company incurred after the conversion takes effect is that of a limited liability company member.

(Added by Stats. 2012, Ch. 419, Sec. 20. Effective January 1, 2013. Operative January 1, 2014, by Sec. 32 of Ch. 419.)

17710.10.

Mergers of limited liability companies shall be governed by Sections 17710.11 to 17710.19, inclusive.

(Added by Stats. 2012, Ch. 419, Sec. 20. Effective January 1, 2013. Operative January 1, 2014, by Sec. 32 of Ch. 419.)

17710.11.

The following entities may be merged pursuant to this article:
(a) Two or more limited liability companies, two or more foreign limited liability companies, or one or more limited liability companies and one or more foreign limited liability companies into one limited liability company or foreign limited liability company except that there must be at least one constituent domestic limited liability company for a surviving limited liability company.
(b) One or more limited liability companies, one or more foreign limited liability companies, and one or more other business entities into one of those other business entities or foreign other business entities.
(c) One or more limited liability companies, one or more foreign limited liability companies, and one or more other business entities or foreign other business entities into one limited liability company or foreign limited liability company.
(d) Notwithstanding this section, the merger of any number of limited liability companies with any number of other business entities or foreign other business entities may be effected only if the other business entities that are organized in this state are authorized by the laws under which they are organized to effect the merger, and the following apply:
  (1) If a limited liability company is the surviving limited liability company, the foreign other business entities are not prohibited by the laws under which they are organized from effecting that merger.
  (2) If a foreign limited liability company or foreign other business entity is the survivor of the merger, the laws of the jurisdiction under which the survivor is organized authorize that merger. Notwithstanding the first sentence of this paragraph, if one or more domestic corporations is also a party to the merger described in that sentence, the merger may be effected only if, with respect to any foreign other business entity that is a corporation, the foreign corporation is authorized by the laws under which it is organized to effect that merger.

(Added by Stats. 2012, Ch. 419, Sec. 20. Effective January 1, 2013. Operative January 1, 2014, by Sec. 32 of Ch. 419.)

17710.12.

(a) Each limited liability company and other business entity that desires to merge shall approve an agreement of merger.
The agreement of merger shall be approved by all managers and a majority in interest of each class of membership interests of each constituent limited liability

ARTICLE 10. Merger and Conversion [17710.01 - 17710.19]

company, unless a greater approval is required by the operating agreement of the constituent limited liability company. Notwithstanding the previous sentence, if the members of any constituent limited liability company become personally liable for any obligations of a constituent limited liability company or constituent other business entity as a result of the merger, the principal terms of the agreement of merger shall be approved by all of the members of the constituent limited liability company, unless the agreement of merger provides that all members shall have the dissenters' rights provided in Article 11 (commencing with Section 17711.01). The agreement of merger shall be approved on behalf of each constituent other business entity by those persons required to approve the merger by the laws under which it is organized. Other persons, including a parent of a constituent limited liability company, may be parties to the agreement of merger. The agreement of merger shall state all of the following:

(1) The terms and conditions of the merger.
(2) The name and place of the organization of the surviving limited liability company or surviving other business entity, and of each disappearing limited liability company and disappearing other business entity, and the agreement of merger may change the name of the surviving limited liability company, the new name may be the same as or similar to the name of a disappearing domestic or foreign limited liability company, subject to Section 17701.08.
(3) The manner of converting the membership interests of each of the constituent limited liability companies into interests, shares, or other securities of the surviving limited liability company or surviving other business entity, and if limited liability company interests of any of the constituent limited liability companies are not to be converted solely into interests, shares, or other securities of the surviving limited liability company or surviving other business entity, the cash, property, rights, interests, or securities that the holders of the limited liability company interests are to receive in exchange for the membership interests, the cash, property, rights, interests, or securities that may be in addition to or in lieu of interests, shares, or other securities of the surviving limited liability company or surviving other business entity, or that the limited liability company interests are canceled without consideration.
(4) The amendments to the articles of organization of the surviving limited liability company, if applicable, to be effected by the merger, if any.
(5) Any other details or provisions that are required by the laws under which any constituent other business entity is organized, including, if a domestic corporation is a party to the merger, as provided in subdivision (b) of Section 1113.
(6) Any other details or provisions that are desired, including, without limitation, a provision for the treatment of fractional membership interests.

(b)
(1) Each membership interest of the same class of any constituent limited liability company, other than a membership interest in another constituent limited liability company that is being canceled and that is held by a constituent limited liability company or its parent or a limited liability company of which the

constituent limited liability company is a parent shall, unless all members of the class consent, be treated equally with respect to any distribution of cash, property, rights, interests, or securities.
  (2) Notwithstanding paragraph (1), except in a merger of a limited liability company with a limited liability company that controls at least 90 percent of the membership interests entitled to vote with respect to the merger, the unredeemable membership interests of a constituent limited liability company may be converted only into unredeemable interests or securities of the surviving limited liability company or other business entity, or a parent if a constituent limited liability company or a constituent other business entity or its parent owns, directly or indirectly, prior to the merger, membership interests of another constituent limited liability company or interests or securities of a constituent other business entity representing more than 50 percent of the interests or securities entitled to vote with respect to the merger of the other constituent limited liability company or constituent other business entity or more than 50 percent of the voting power, as defined in Section 194.5, of a constituent other business entity that is a domestic corporation, unless all of the members of the class consent.
  (3) The provisions of this subdivision do not apply to any transaction if the commissioner has approved the terms and conditions of the transaction and the fairness of those terms pursuant to Section 25142.
(c) Notwithstanding its prior approval, an agreement of merger may be amended prior to the filing of the certificate of merger or the agreement of merger, as provided in Section 17710.14, if the amendment is approved by the managers and members of each constituent limited liability company in the same manner as required for approval of the original agreement of merger and, if the amendment changes any of the principal terms of the agreement of merger, the amendment is approved by the managers and members of each constituent limited liability company in the same manner and to the same extent as required for the approval of the original agreement of merger, and by each of the constituent other business entities.
(d) The managers and members of a constituent limited liability company may, in their discretion, abandon a merger, subject to the contractual rights, if any, of third parties, including other constituent limited liability companies and constituent other business entities, without further approval by the membership interests, at any time before the merger is effective.
(e) An agreement of merger approved in accordance with subdivision (a) may do the following:
  (1) Effect any amendment to the operating agreement of any constituent limited liability company.
  (2) Effect the adoption of a new operating agreement for a constituent limited liability company if it is the surviving limited liability company in the merger. Any amendment to an operating agreement or adoption of a new operating agreement made pursuant to the foregoing sentence shall be effective at the effective time or date of the merger. Notwithstanding the above provisions of this subdivision, if a greater number of members is required to approve an

ARTICLE 10. *Merger and Conversion [17710.01 - 17710.19]*

amendment to the operating agreement of a constituent limited liability company than is required to approve the agreement of merger pursuant to subdivision (a), and the number of members that approve the agreement of merger is less than the number of members required to approve an amendment to the operating agreement of the constituent limited liability company, any amendment to the operating agreement or adoption of a new operating agreement of that constituent limited liability company made pursuant to the first sentence of this subdivision shall be effective only if the agreement of merger provides that all of the members shall have the dissenters' rights provided in Article 11 (commencing with Section 17711.01).

(f) The surviving limited liability company or surviving other business entity shall keep the agreement of merger at its designated office or at the business address specified in paragraph (5) of subdivision (a) of Section 17710.14, as applicable, and, upon the request of a member of a constituent limited liability company or a holder of shares, interests, or other securities of a constituent other business entity, the managers or members of the surviving limited liability company or the authorized person of the surviving other business entity shall promptly deliver to the member or the holder of shares, interests, or other securities, at the expense of the surviving limited liability company or surviving other business entity, a copy of the agreement of merger. A waiver by a member or holder of shares, interests, or other securities of the rights provided in this subdivision shall be unenforceable.

(Added by Stats. 2012, Ch. 419, Sec. 20. Effective January 1, 2013. Operative January 1, 2014, by Sec. 32 of Ch. 419.)

17710.13.

Subdivision (b) of Section 17710.12 shall not apply to any transaction if the commissioner has approved the terms and conditions of the transaction and the fairness of such terms and conditions pursuant to Section 25142.

(Added by Stats. 2012, Ch. 419, Sec. 20. Effective January 1, 2013. Operative January 1, 2014, by Sec. 32 of Ch. 419.)

17710.14.

(a) If the surviving entity is a limited liability company or an other business entity, other than a corporation in a merger in which a domestic corporation is a constituent party, after approval of a merger by the constituent limited liability companies and any constituent other business entities, the constituent limited liability companies and constituent other business entities shall file a certificate of merger in the office of, and on a form prescribed by, the Secretary of State. The certificate of merger shall be executed and acknowledged by each domestic constituent limited liability company by all managers, or if none, all members unless a lesser number is provided in the articles of organization or operating agreement of the domestic constituent limited liability company and by each foreign constituent limited liability company by one or more managers, or if none, members, and by each constituent other business entity by those persons required to execute the certificate of merger by the laws under which the constituent other business entity is organized. The certificate of merger shall set forth all of the following:

(1) The names and the Secretary of State's file numbers, if any, of each of the constituent limited liability companies and constituent other business entities, separately identifying the disappearing limited liability companies and disappearing other business entities and the surviving limited liability company or surviving other business entity.

(2) If a vote of the members was required pursuant to Section 17710.12, a statement setting forth the total number of outstanding interests of each class entitled to vote on the merger and that the principal terms of the agreement of merger were approved by a vote of the number of interests of each class that equaled or exceeded the vote required, specifying each class entitled to vote and the percentage vote required of each class.

(3) If the surviving entity is a limited liability company and not an other business entity, any change required to the information set forth in the articles of organization of the surviving limited liability company resulting from the merger, including any change in the name of the surviving limited liability company resulting from the merger. The filing of a certificate of merger setting forth any such changes to the articles of organization of the surviving limited liability company shall have the effect of the filing of a certificate of amendment by the surviving limited liability company, and the surviving limited liability company need not file an amendment under Section 17702.02 to reflect those changes.

(4) The future effective date, that shall be a date certain not more than 90 days subsequent to the date of filing of the merger, if the merger is not to be effective upon the filing of the certificate of merger with the office of the Secretary of State.

(5) If the surviving entity is an other business entity or a foreign limited liability company, the full name of the entity, type of entity, legal jurisdiction where the entity was organized and by whose laws its internal affairs are governed, and the address of the principal place of business of the entity.

(6) Any other information required to be stated in the certificate of merger by the laws where each constituent other business entity is organized, including if a domestic corporation is a party to the merger, as required under paragraph (2) of subdivision (g) of Section 1113. If the surviving entity is a foreign limited liability company in a merger where a domestic corporation is a disappearing other business entity, a copy of the agreement of merger and attachments as required under paragraph (1) of subdivision (g) of Section 1113 shall be filed at the same time as the filing of the certificate of merger.

(b) If the surviving entity is a domestic corporation or a foreign corporation in a merger that a domestic corporation is a constituent party, after approval of the merger by the constituent limited liability companies and constituent other business entities, the surviving corporation shall file in the office of the Secretary of State a copy of the

ARTICLE 10. Merger and Conversion [17710.01 - 17710.19]

agreement of merger and attachments required under paragraph (1) of subdivision (g) of Section 1113. The certificate of merger shall be executed and acknowledged by each domestic constituent limited liability company by all general members, unless a lesser number is provided in the articles of organization of the limited liability company of the domestic constituent limited liability company.

(c) A certificate of merger or the agreement of merger, as is applicable under subdivisions (a) and (b), shall have the effect of the filing of a certificate of cancellation for each disappearing limited liability company, and no disappearing limited liability company need take any action under Article 7 (commencing with Section 17707.01) concerning dissolution as a result of the merger.

(d) If a disappearing other entity is a foreign corporation qualified to transact intrastate business in this state, the filing of the certificate of merger or agreement of merger, as is applicable, by the foreign corporation shall automatically surrender its right to transact intrastate business.

(Added by Stats. 2012, Ch. 419, Sec. 20. Effective January 1, 2013. Operative January 1, 2014, by Sec. 32 of Ch. 419.)

17710.15.

(a) Unless a future effective date is provided in a certificate of merger or the agreement of merger, if an agreement of merger is required to be filed under Section 17710.14, in which event the merger shall be effective at that future effective date, a merger shall be effective upon the filing of the certificate of merger or the agreement of merger, as is applicable, in the office of the Secretary of State.

(b)

   (1) For all purposes, a copy of the certificate of merger duly certified by the Secretary of State is conclusive evidence of the merger of the constituent limited liability companies, either by themselves or together with constituent other business entities, into the surviving other business entity, or the constituent limited liability companies or the constituent other business entities, or both, into the surviving limited liability company.

   (2) In a merger in which the surviving entity is a corporation in a merger in which a domestic corporation and a domestic limited liability company are parties to the merger, a copy of an agreement of merger certified on or after the effective date by an official having custody thereof has the same force in evidence as the original and, except as against the state, is conclusive evidence of the performance of all conditions precedent to the merger, the existence on the effective date of the surviving corporation, and the performance of the conditions necessary to the adoption of any amendment to the articles of incorporation of the surviving corporation, if applicable, contained in the agreement of merger.

(Added by Stats. 2012, Ch. 419, Sec. 20. Effective January 1, 2013. Operative January 1, 2014, by Sec. 32 of Ch. 419.)

17710.16.

(a) Upon a merger of limited liability companies or limited liability companies and other business entities pursuant to this article, the separate existence of the disappearing limited liability companies and disappearing other business entities ceases and the surviving limited liability company or surviving other business entity shall succeed, without other transfer, act or deed, to all the rights and property, whether real, personal, or mixed, of each of the disappearing limited liability companies and disappearing other business entities, and shall be subject to all the debts and liabilities of each in the same manner as if the surviving limited liability company or surviving other business entity had itself incurred them.

(b) All rights of creditors and all liens upon the property of each of the constituent limited liability companies and constituent other business entities shall be preserved unimpaired and may be enforced against the surviving limited liability company or the surviving other business entity to the same extent as if the debt, liability, or duty which gave rise to that lien had been incurred or contracted by the surviving limited liability company or the surviving other business entity, provided that such liens upon the property of a disappearing limited liability company or disappearing other business entity shall be limited to the property affected thereby immediately prior to the time the merger is effective.

(c) Any action or proceeding pending by or against any disappearing limited liability company or disappearing other business entity may be prosecuted to judgment, which shall bind the surviving limited liability company or surviving other business entity, or the surviving limited liability company or surviving other business entity may be proceeded against or be substituted in the place of the disappearing limited liability company or disappearing other business entity.

(d) Nothing in this article is intended to affect the liability a member of a disappearing limited liability company may have in connection with the debts and liabilities of the disappearing limited liability company existing prior to the time the merger is effective.

(Added by Stats. 2012, Ch. 419, Sec. 20. Effective January 1, 2013. Operative January 1, 2014, by Sec. 32 of Ch. 419.)

17710.17.

(a) If the surviving entity is a domestic limited liability company or a domestic other business entity, the merger proceedings with respect to that limited liability company or other business entity and any domestic disappearing limited liability company shall conform to the provisions of this article governing the merger of domestic limited liability companies, but if the surviving entity is a foreign limited liability company or a foreign other business entity, then, subject to the requirements of subdivision (d) and Article 11 (commencing with Section 17711.01) and, with respect to any domestic constituent corporation, Section 1113, Chapter 12 (commencing with Section 1200), and Chapter 13 (commencing with Section 1300) of Division 1 of Title 1 and, with respect to any domestic constituent limited

ARTICLE 10. Merger and Conversion [17710.01 - 17710.19]

partnership, Article 11.5 (commencing with Section 15911.20) of Chapter 5.5 of Title 2, the merger proceedings may be in accordance with the laws of the state or place of organization of the surviving limited liability company or surviving other business entity.

(b) If the surviving entity is a domestic limited liability company or domestic other business entity, other than a domestic corporation, the certificate of merger shall be filed as provided in subdivision (a) of Section 17710.14, and thereupon, subject to subdivision (a) of Section 17710.15, the merger shall be effective as to each domestic constituent limited liability company and domestic constituent other business entity. If the surviving entity is a domestic corporation, the agreement of merger with attachments shall be filed pursuant to subdivision (b) of Section 17710.14, and thereupon, subject to subdivision (a) of Section 17710.15, the merger shall be effective as to each domestic constituent limited liability company and domestic constituent other business entity unless another effective date is provided pursuant to Article 11 (commencing with Section 17711.01), with respect to any constituent corporation or constituent limited liability company.

(c) If the surviving entity is a foreign limited liability company or foreign other business entity, the merger shall become effective in accordance with the laws of the jurisdiction where the surviving limited liability company or surviving other business entity is organized, but shall be effective as to any domestic disappearing limited liability company as of the time of effectiveness in the foreign jurisdiction upon the filing in this state of a certificate of merger or agreement of merger pursuant to Section 17710.14.

(d) If a merger described in subdivision (c) or (d) also includes a foreign disappearing limited liability company previously registered for the transaction of intrastate business in this state pursuant to Section 17708.02, the filing of the certificate of merger or agreement of merger, as is applicable under Section 17710.14, automatically has the effect of a cancellation of registration for that foreign limited liability company pursuant to Section 17708.07 without the necessity of the filing of a certificate of cancellation.

(e) The provisions of subdivision (b) of Section 17710.12 and Article 11 (commencing with Section 17711.01) apply to the rights of the members of any of the constituent limited liability companies that are domestic limited liability companies and of any domestic limited liability company that is a parent of any foreign constituent limited liability company.

(f) If the surviving entity is a foreign limited liability company or foreign other business entity, the surviving entity shall file the following with the Secretary of State:
   (1) An agreement that it may be served in this state in a proceeding for the enforcement of an obligation of any constituent entity and in a proceeding to enforce the rights of any holder of a dissenting interest or dissenting shares in a constituent domestic limited liability company or domestic other business entity.
   (2) An irrevocable appointment of the Secretary of State as its agent for service of process, and an address to which process may be forwarded.
   (3) An agreement that it will promptly pay the holder of any dissenting interest or dissenting share in a constituent domestic limited liability company or domestic

other business entity the amount to which that person is entitled under the laws of this state.

(Added by Stats. 2012, Ch. 419, Sec. 20. Effective January 1, 2013. Operative January 1, 2014, by Sec. 32 of Ch. 419.)

17710.18.

Whenever a domestic or foreign limited liability company or other business entity having any real property in this state merges with another limited liability company or other business entity pursuant to the laws of this state or of the state or place where any constituent limited liability company or constituent other business entity was organized, and the laws of the state or place of organization, including this state of any disappearing limited liability company or disappearing other business entity provide substantially that the making and filing of the agreement of merger or certificate of merger vests in the surviving limited liability company or surviving other business entity all the real property of any disappearing limited liability company and disappearing other business entity, the filing for record in the office of the county recorder of any county in this state where any of the real property of the disappearing limited liability company or disappearing other business entity is located of either of the following shall evidence record ownership in the surviving limited liability company or surviving other business entity of all interest of the disappearing limited liability company or disappearing other business entity in and to the real property located in that county in which both of the following occur:
(a) A certificate of merger certified by the Secretary of State, or other certificate prescribed by the Secretary of State.
(b) A copy of the agreement of merger or certificate of merger, certified by the Secretary of State or an authorized public official of the state or place pursuant to the laws of which the merger is effected.

(Added by Stats. 2012, Ch. 419, Sec. 20. Effective January 1, 2013. Operative January 1, 2014, by Sec. 32 of Ch. 419.)

17710.19.

(a) Upon a merger pursuant to this article, a surviving domestic or foreign limited liability company or other business entity shall be deemed to have assumed the liability of each disappearing domestic or foreign limited liability company or other business entity that is taxed under Part 10 (commencing with Section 17001) or Part 11 (commencing with Section 23001) of Division 2 of the Revenue and Taxation Code for the following:
   (1) To prepare and file, or to cause to be prepared and filed, tax and information returns otherwise required of that disappearing entity as specified in Chapter 2 (commencing with Section 18501) of Part 10.2 of Division 2 of the Revenue and Taxation Code.
   (2) To pay any tax liability determined to be due.

(b) If the surviving entity is a domestic limited liability company, domestic corporation, or registered limited liability partnership or a foreign limited liability company, foreign limited liability partnership, or foreign corporation that is registered or qualified to do business in this state, the Secretary of State shall notify the Franchise Tax Board of the merger.

(Added by Stats. 2012, Ch. 419, Sec. 20. Effective January 1, 2013. Operative January 1, 2014, by Sec. 32 of Ch. 419.)

ARTICLE 11. Dissenters' Rights [17711.01 - 17711.14]

17711.01.

(a) For purposes of this article, "reorganization" refers to any of the following:
   (1) A conversion pursuant to Article 10 (commencing with Section 17710.01).
   (2) A merger pursuant to Article 10 (commencing with Section 17710.01).
   (3) The acquisition by one limited liability company in exchange, in whole or in part, for its membership interests, or the membership interests or equity securities of a limited liability company or other business entity that is in control of the acquiring limited liability company, of membership interests or equity securities of another limited liability company or other business entity if, immediately after the acquisition, the acquiring limited liability company has control of the other limited liability company or other business entity.
   (4) The acquisition by one limited liability company in exchange, in whole or in part, for its membership interests, or the membership interests or equity securities of a limited liability company or other business entity which is in control of the acquiring limited liability company, or for its debt securities, or debt securities of a limited liability company or other business entity which is in control of the acquiring limited liability company, that are not adequately secured and that have a maturity date in excess of five years after the consummation of the acquisition, or both, of all or substantially all of the assets of another limited liability company or other business entity.
(b) For purposes of this article, "control" means the possession, direct or indirect, of the power to direct or cause the direction of the management and policies of a limited liability company or other business entity.

(Added by Stats. 2012, Ch. 419, Sec. 20. Effective January 1, 2013. Operative January 1, 2014, by Sec. 32 of Ch. 419.)

17711.02.

(a) If the approval of outstanding membership interests is required for a limited liability company to participate in a reorganization, pursuant to the limited liability company agreement, or otherwise, then each member of the limited liability company holding those interests may, by complying with this article, require the limited liability company to purchase for cash, at its fair market value, the interest owned by the member in the limited liability company, if the interest is a dissenting interest as defined in subdivision (b). The fair market value shall be determined as of the day before the first announcement of the terms of the proposed reorganization, excluding any appreciation or depreciation in consequence of the proposed reorganization.

(b) As used in this article, "dissenting interest" means the interest of a member that satisfies all of the following conditions:
  (1) Either:
      (A) Was not, immediately prior to the reorganization, either (i) listed on any national securities exchange certified by the Commissioner of Corporations under subdivision (o) of Section 25100, or (ii) listed on the list of OTC margin stocks issued by the Board of Governors of the Federal Reserve System, provided that in either instance the limited liability company whose outstanding interests are so listed provides, in its notice to members requesting their approval of the proposed reorganization, a summary of the provisions of this section and Sections 17711.03, 17711.04, 17711.05, and 17711.06.
      (B) If the interest is of a class of interests listed as described in clause (i) or (ii) of subparagraph (A), demands for payment are filed with respect to 5 percent or more of the outstanding interests of that class.
  (2) Was outstanding on the date for the determination of members entitled to vote on the reorganization.
  (3) Either:
      (A) Was not voted in favor of the reorganization.
      (B) If the interest is described in clause (i) or (ii) of subparagraph (A) of paragraph (1), was voted against the reorganization; provided, however, that subparagraph (A) rather than this subparagraph applies in any event where the approval for the proposed reorganization is sought by written consent rather than at a meeting.
  (4) The member has demanded that the interest be purchased by the limited liability company at its fair market value in accordance with Section 17711.03.
  (5) The member has submitted the interest for endorsement, if applicable, in accordance with Section 17711.04.
(c) As used in this article, "dissenting member" means the recordholder of a dissenting interest, and includes an assignee of record of that interest.

(Added by Stats. 2012, Ch. 419, Sec. 20. Effective January 1, 2013. Operative January 1, 2014, by Sec. 32 of Ch. 419.)

17711.03.

(a) If members have a right under Section 17711.02, subject to compliance with paragraphs (4) and (5) of subdivision (b) of Section 17711.02, to require the limited liability company to purchase their membership interests for cash, the limited liability company shall mail to each member a notice of the approval of the reorganization by the requisite vote or consent of the members, within 10 days after the date of the approval, accompanied by a copy of this section and Sections 17711.01, 17711.02, 17711.04, and 17711.05, a statement of the price determined by the limited liability company to represent the fair market value of its outstanding interests, and a brief description of the procedure to be followed if the member desires to exercise the member's rights under those sections. The statement of price constitutes an offer by the limited liability company to purchase at the price stated any dissenting interests as defined in subdivision (b) of Section 17711.02, unless they lose their status as dissenting interests under Section 17711.11.

(b) Any member who has a right to require the limited liability company to purchase the member's interest for cash under Section 17711.02, subject to compliance with paragraphs (4) and (5) of subdivision (b) of Section 17711.02, and who desires the limited liability company to purchase that interest, shall make written demand upon the limited liability company for the purchase of that interest and the payment to the member in cash of its fair market value. The demand is not effective for any purpose unless it is received by the limited liability company or any transfer agent thereof (1) in the case of interests described in clause (i) or (ii) of subparagraph (A) of paragraph (1) of subdivision (b) of Section 17711.02, not later than the date of the members' meeting to vote upon the reorganization, or (2) in any other case, within 30 days after the date on which notice of the approval of the reorganization by the requisite vote or consent of the members is mailed by the limited liability company to the members.

(c) The demand shall state the number or amount of the member's interest in the limited liability company and shall contain a statement of what the member claims to be the fair market value of that interest on the day before the announcement of the proposed reorganization. The statement of fair market value constitutes an offer by the member to sell the interest at such price.

(Added by Stats. 2012, Ch. 419, Sec. 20. Effective January 1, 2013. Operative January 1, 2014, by Sec. 32 of Ch. 419.)

17711.04.

Within 30 days after the date on which notice of the approval of the outstanding interests of the limited liability company is mailed to the member pursuant to subdivision (a) of Section 17711.03, the member shall submit to the limited liability company at its principal office or at the office of any transfer agent thereof, if the interest is evidenced by a certificate, the member's certificate representing the interest which the member demands that the limited liability company purchase, to be stamped or endorsed with a statement that the interest is a dissenting interest or to be exchanged for certificates of appropriate denominations so stamped or endorsed, or if the interest is not evidenced by a certificate, written notice of the number or amount of interest which the member demands that the limited liability company purchase. Upon subsequent transfers of the dissenting interest on the books of the limited liability company, the new certificates or other written statement issued therefor shall bear a like statement, together with the name of the original holder of the dissenting interest.

(Added by Stats. 2012, Ch. 419, Sec. 20. Effective January 1, 2013. Operative January 1, 2014, by Sec. 32 of Ch. 419.)

17711.05.

(a) If the limited liability company and the dissenting member agree that the member's interest is a dissenting interest and agree upon the price to be paid for the dissenting interest, the dissenting member is entitled to the agreed price with interest thereon at the legal rate on judgments from the date of consummation of the reorganization. All agreements fixing the fair market value of any dissenting member's interest as between the limited liability company and that member shall be in writing and filed in the records of the limited liability company.

(b) Subject to the provisions of Section 17711.08, payment of the fair market value for a dissenting interest shall be made within 30 days after the amount has been agreed to or within 30 days after any statutory or contractual conditions to the reorganization are satisfied, whichever is later, and in the case of dissenting interests evidenced by certificates of interest, subject to surrender of such certificates of interest, unless provided otherwise by agreement.

(Added by Stats. 2012, Ch. 419, Sec. 20. Effective January 1, 2013. Operative January 1, 2014, by Sec. 32 of Ch. 419.)

17711.06.

(a) If the limited liability company denies that a membership interest is a dissenting interest, or the limited liability company and a dissenting member fail to agree upon the fair market value of a dissenting interest, then the member or any interested limited liability company, within six months after the date when notice of the approval of the reorganization by the requisite vote or consent of the members was mailed to the member, but not later, may file a complaint in the superior court of the proper county praying the court to determine whether the interest is a dissenting interest, or the fair market value of the dissenting interest, or both, or may intervene in any action pending on such a complaint.

(b) Two or more dissenting members may join as plaintiffs or be joined as defendants in any of those actions and two or more of those actions may be consolidated.

(c) On the trial of the action, the court shall determine the issues. If the status of the membership interest as a dissenting interest is in issue, the court shall first determine that issue. If the fair market value of the dissenting interest is in issue, the court shall determine, or shall appoint one or more impartial appraisers to determine, the fair market value of the dissenting interest.

(Added by Stats. 2012, Ch. 419, Sec. 20. Effective January 1, 2013. Operative January 1, 2014, by Sec. 32 of Ch. 419.)

17711.07.

(a) If the court appoints an appraiser or appraisers, they shall proceed forthwith to determine the fair market value per interest of the outstanding membership interests of the limited liability company, by class if necessary. Within the time fixed by the court, the appraisers, or a majority of them, shall make and file a report in the office of the clerk of the court. Thereupon, on the motion of any party, the report shall be submitted to the court and considered on such additional evidence as the court considers relevant. If the court finds the report reasonable, the court may confirm it.
(b) If a majority of the appraisers appointed fails to make and file a report within 30 days from the date of their appointment, or within a further time as may be allowed by the court, or the report is not confirmed by the court, the court shall determine the fair market value per interest of the outstanding membership interests of the limited liability company, by class if necessary.
(c) Subject to Section 17711.08, judgment shall be rendered against the limited liability company for payment of an amount equal to the fair market value, as determined by the court, of each dissenting interest that any dissenting member who is a party, or has intervened, is entitled to require the limited liability company to purchase, with interest thereon at the legal rate on judgments from the date of consummation of the reorganization.
(d) Any of those judgments shall be payable forthwith, provided, however, that with respect to membership interests evidenced by transferable certificates of interest, only upon the endorsement and delivery to the limited liability company of those certificates representing the interests described in the judgment. Any party may appeal from the judgment.
(e) The costs of the action, including reasonable compensation for the appraisers, to be fixed by the court, shall be assessed or apportioned as the court considers equitable, but, if the appraisal exceeds the price offered by the limited liability company, the limited liability company shall pay the costs, including, in the discretion of the court, if the value awarded by the court for the dissenting interest is more than 125 percent of the price offered by the limited liability company under subdivision (a) of Section 17711.02, attorney's fees and fees of expert witnesses.

(Added by Stats. 2012, Ch. 419, Sec. 20. Effective January 1, 2013. Operative January 1, 2014, by Sec. 32 of Ch. 419.)

17711.08.

To the extent that the payment to dissenting members of the fair market value of their dissenting interests would require the dissenting members to return payment or a portion of the payment by reason of Section 17711.09 or the Uniform Fraudulent Transfer Act (Chapter 1 (commencing with Section 3439) of Title 2 of Part 2 of Division 4 of the Civil Code), then that payment or portion thereof shall not be made and the dissenting members shall become creditors of the limited liability company for the amount not paid, together with interest thereon at the legal rate on judgments until the date of payment, but subordinate to all other creditors in any proceeding relating to the winding up and dissolution of the limited liability company, such debt to be payable when permissible.

(Added by Stats. 2012, Ch. 419, Sec. 20. Effective January 1, 2013. Operative January 1, 2014, by Sec. 32 of Ch. 419.)

17711.09.

Any cash distributions made by a limited liability company to a dissenting member after the date of consummation of the reorganization, but prior to any payment by the limited liability company for that dissenting member's interest, shall be credited against the total amount to be paid by the limited liability company for such dissenting interest.

(Added by Stats. 2012, Ch. 419, Sec. 20. Effective January 1, 2013. Operative January 1, 2014, by Sec. 32 of Ch. 419.)

17711.10.

Except as expressly limited by this article, dissenting members shall continue to have all the rights and privileges incident to their interests immediately prior to the reorganization, including limited liability, until payment by the limited liability company for their dissenting interests. A dissenting member may not withdraw a demand for payment unless the limited liability company consents thereto.

(Added by Stats. 2012, Ch. 419, Sec. 20. Effective January 1, 2013. Operative January 1, 2014, by Sec. 32 of Ch. 419.)

17711.11.

A dissenting interest loses its status as a dissenting interest and the holder thereof ceases to be a dissenting member and ceases to be entitled to require the limited liability company to purchase the interest upon the happening of any of the following:
(a) The limited liability company abandons the reorganization.
 Upon abandonment of the reorganization, the limited liability company shall pay, on demand, to any dissenting member who has initiated proceeding in good faith under this article, all reasonable expenses incurred in such proceedings and reasonable attorney's fees.
(b) The interest is transferred prior to its submission for endorsement in accordance with Section 17711.04.
(c) The dissenting member and the limited liability company do not agree upon the status of the interest as a dissenting interest or upon the purchase price of the dissenting interest, and neither files a complaint nor intervenes in a pending action, as provided in Section 17711.06, within six months after the date upon which notice of the approval of the reorganization by the requisite vote or consent of members was mailed to the member.

ARTICLE 11. Dissenters' Rights [17711.01 - 17711.14]

(d) The dissenting member, with the consent of the limited liability company, withdraws the member's demand for purchase of the dissenting interest.

(Added by Stats. 2012, Ch. 419, Sec. 20. Effective January 1, 2013. Operative January 1, 2014, by Sec. 32 of Ch. 419.)

17711.12.

If litigation is instituted to test the sufficiency or regularity of the vote or consent of the members in authorizing a reorganization, any proceedings under Sections 17711.06 and 17711.07 shall be suspended until final determination of that litigation.

(Added by Stats. 2012, Ch. 419, Sec. 20. Effective January 1, 2013. Operative January 1, 2014, by Sec. 32 of Ch. 419.)

17711.13.

(a) This article applies to the following:
   (1) A domestic limited liability company formed on or after January 1, 2014.
   (2) A foreign limited liability company if the foreign limited liability company was formed on or after January 1, 2014, or filed an application to qualify to do business on or after January 1, 2014, and members holding more than 50 percent of the voting power held by all members of the foreign limited liability company reside in this state.
   (3) A limited liability company if the operating agreement so provides or if all managers and a majority of the members, if it is a manager-managed limited liability company, or a majority, if it is a member-managed limited liability company, determine that this article shall apply.
(b) This article does not apply to membership interests governed by operating agreements whose terms and provisions specifically set forth the amount to be paid in respect of those interests in the event of a reorganization of the limited liability company, or to any limited liability company with 35 or fewer members if all the members have waived the application of this article in writing, whether in an operating agreement or otherwise, provided that if, at the time of the reorganization, the limited liability company had more than 35 members, any waiver shall be ineffective as to that reorganization.

(Added by Stats. 2012, Ch. 419, Sec. 20. Effective January 1, 2013. Operative January 1, 2014, by Sec. 32 of Ch. 419.)

17711.14.

(a) No member of a limited liability company who has a right under this article to demand payment of cash for the interest owned by a member in a limited liability company shall have any right at law or in equity to attack the validity of the reorganization, or to have the reorganization set aside or rescinded, except in an action to test whether the vote or consent of members required to authorize or

approve the reorganization has been obtained in accordance with the procedures established therefor by the operating agreement of the limited liability company.
(b) If one of the parties to a reorganization is directly or indirectly controlled by, or under common control with, another party to the reorganization, subdivision (a) shall not apply to any member of the controlled party who has not demanded payment of cash for the member's interest pursuant to this article; but if the member institutes any action to attack the validity of the reorganization or to have the reorganization set aside or rescinded, the member shall not thereafter have any right to demand payment of cash for the member's interest pursuant to this article.
(c) If one of the parties to a reorganization is directly or indirectly controlled by, or under common control with, another party to the reorganization, then, in any action to attack the validity of the reorganization or to have the reorganization set aside or rescinded, both of the following apply:
  (1) A party to a reorganization that controls another party to a reorganization shall have the burden of proving that the transaction is just and reasonable as to the members of the controlled party.
  (2) A person that controls two or more parties to a reorganization shall have the burden of proving that the transaction is just and reasonable as to the members of any party so controlled.
(d) Subdivisions (b) and (c) shall not apply if a majority of the members other than members who are directly or indirectly controlled by, or under common control with, another party to the reorganization approve or consent to the reorganization.
(e) This section shall not prevent a member of a limited liability company that is a party to a reorganization from bringing an action against a manager of the limited liability company, the limited liability company, or any person controlling a manager at law or in equity as to any matters, including, without limitation, an action for breach of fiduciary obligation or fraud, other than to attack the validity of the reorganization or to have the reorganization set aside or rescinded.

(Added by Stats. 2012, Ch. 419, Sec. 20. Effective January 1, 2013. Operative January 1, 2014, by Sec. 32 of Ch. 419.)

ARTICLE 12. Class Provisions [17712.01- 17712.01.]

17712.01.

The articles of organization or the operating agreement may provide for the creation of classes of members having those relative rights, powers, and duties as the articles of organization or operating agreement may provide, including rights, powers, and duties senior to other classes of members.

(Added by Stats. 2012, Ch. 419, Sec. 20. Effective January 1, 2013. Operative January 1, 2014, by Sec. 32 of Ch. 419.)

ARTICLE 13. Miscellaneous Provisions [17713.01 - 17713.13]

17713.01.

In applying and construing this uniform act, consideration shall be given to the need to promote uniformity of the law with respect to its subject matter among states that enact it.

(Added by Stats. 2012, Ch. 419, Sec. 20. Effective January 1, 2013. Operative January 1, 2014, by Sec. 32 of Ch. 419.)

17713.02.

This title modifies, limits, and supersedes the federal Electronic Signatures in Global and National Commerce Act (15 U.S.C. Sec. 7001 et seq.), but does not modify, limit, or supersede Section 101(c) of that act (15 U.S.C. Sec. 7001(c)), or authorize electronic delivery of any of the notices described in Section 103(b) of that act (15 U.S.C. Sec. 7003(b)).

(Added by Stats. 2012, Ch. 419, Sec. 20. Effective January 1, 2013. Operative January 1, 2014, by Sec. 32 of Ch. 419.)

17713.03.

This title does not affect an action commenced, proceeding brought, or right accrued or accruing before this title takes effect.

(Added by Stats. 2012, Ch. 419, Sec. 20. Effective January 1, 2013. Operative January 1, 2014, by Sec. 32 of Ch. 419.)

17713.04.

(a) Except as otherwise specified in this title, this title shall apply to all domestic limited liability companies existing on or after January 1, 2014, to all foreign limited liability companies registered with the Secretary of State prior to January 1, 2014, whose registrations have not been canceled as of January 1, 2014, to all foreign limited liability companies registered with the Secretary of State on or after January 1, 2014, and to all actions taken by the managers or members of a limited liability company on or after that date.

(b) Except as otherwise specified in this title, this title applies only to the acts or transactions by a limited liability company or by the members or managers of the limited liability company occurring, or contracts entered into by the limited liability company or by the members or managers of the limited liability company, on or after January 1, 2014. The prior law governs all acts or transactions by a limited liability company or by the members or managers of the limited liability company occurring, or contracts entered into by the limited liability company or by the members or managers of the limited liability company, prior to that date.

(c) Except as otherwise specified in this title, any vote or consent by the managers or members of a limited liability company prior to January 1, 2014, shall be governed by prior law. If a certificate or document is required to be filed in a public office of this state relating to a vote or consent by the managers or members of the limited liability company prior to January 1, 2014, it may be filed after that date pursuant to the filing requirements of this title, even though the vote or consent is governed by prior law.

(d) This title does not cancel or otherwise affect the status of, or create a new filing requirement with the Secretary of State or any other agency, board, commission, or department for, any domestic limited liability company in existence on December 31, 2013, or any foreign limited liability company registered to transact intrastate business in this state prior to January 1, 2014.

(e) For the purposes of this section, "prior law" means Title 2.5 (commencing with Section 17000) as it read on December 31, 2013.

(Added by Stats. 2012, Ch. 419, Sec. 20. Effective January 1, 2013. Operative January 1, 2014, by Sec. 32 of Ch. 419.)

17713.05.

This title, or any division, part, chapter, article, or section thereof, may at any time be amended or repealed.

(Added by Stats. 2012, Ch. 419, Sec. 20. Effective January 1, 2013. Operative January 1, 2014, by Sec. 32 of Ch. 419.)

17713.06.

(a) If a manager or member required by this title to execute or file any document fails, after demand, to do so within a reasonable time or refuses to do so, any other manager or member, or any person appointed by a court of competent jurisdiction, may prepare, execute, and file that document with the Secretary of State.

(b) If there is any dispute concerning the filing of a document, or the failure to file a document, any manager or member may petition the superior court to direct the execution of the document.

(c) If the court finds that it is proper for the document to be executed and that any person so designated has failed or refused to execute the document, or if the court determines that any document should be filed, it shall order a party to file the document, on a form prescribed by the Secretary of State if appropriate, as ordered by the court.

(d) In any action under this section, if the court finds the failure of the manager or member to comply with the requirement to file any document to have been without justification, the court may award an amount sufficient to reimburse the managers or members bringing the action for the reasonable expenses incurred by them, including attorney's fees, in connection with the action or proceeding.

(e) Any member who is not a manager, or any person filing any document under this section, shall state the statutory authority after the signature on the appropriate document.

(Added by Stats. 2012, Ch. 419, Sec. 20. Effective January 1, 2013. Operative January 1, 2014, by Sec. 32 of Ch. 419.)

17713.07.

(a) Every limited liability company that neglects, fails, or refuses to keep or cause to be kept or maintained the documents, books, and records required by Section 17701.13 to be kept or maintained shall be subject to a penalty of twenty-five dollars ($25) for each day that the failure or refusal continues, beginning 30 days after receipt of written request by any member that the duty be performed, up to a maximum of one thousand five hundred dollars ($1,500). The penalty shall be paid to the member or members jointly making the request for performance of the duty and damaged by the neglect, failure, or refusal, if suit therefor is commenced within 90 days after the written request is made; but the maximum daily penalty because of failure to comply with any number of separate requests made on any one day or for the same act shall be two hundred fifty dollars ($250).

(b) Upon the failure of a limited liability company, or a foreign limited liability company registered to transact intrastate business in this state, to file the statement required by Section 17702.09, the Secretary of State shall provide a notice of that delinquency to the limited liability company or foreign limited liability company. The notice shall also contain information concerning the application of this section, advise the limited liability company or foreign limited liability company of the penalty imposed by this subdivision for failure to timely file the required statement after notice of delinquency has been provided by the Secretary of State, and shall advise the limited liability company or foreign limited liability company of its right to request relief from the Secretary of State because of reasonable cause or unusual circumstances that justify the failure to file. If, within 60 days after providing notice of the delinquency, a statement pursuant to Section 17702.09 has not been filed by the limited liability company or foreign limited liability company, the limited liability company or foreign limited liability company shall be subject to a penalty of two hundred fifty dollars ($250).

(Added by Stats. 2012, Ch. 419, Sec. 20. Effective January 1, 2013. Operative January 1, 2014, by Sec. 32 of Ch. 419.)

17713.08.

Any penalty prescribed by Section 17713.07 shall be in addition to any remedy by injunction or action for damages or by writ of mandate for the nonperformance of acts and duties enjoined by law upon the limited liability company or its managers, including, without limitation, the remedies provided in subdivisions (f) and (g) of Section 17704.10. The court in which an action for any penalty is brought may reduce, remit, or suspend the penalty on any terms and conditions as it may deem reasonable when it is made to appear that the neglect, failure, or refusal was inadvertent or excusable.

(Added by Stats. 2012, Ch. 419, Sec. 20. Effective January 1, 2013. Operative January 1, 2014, by Sec. 32 of Ch. 419.)

17713.09.

(a) Upon the failure of a limited liability company to file the statement required by Section 17702.09, the Secretary of State shall provide a notice of the delinquency to the limited liability company. The notice shall also contain information concerning the application of this section, advise the limited liability company of the penalty imposed by Section 19141 of the Revenue and Taxation Code for failure to timely file the required statement after notice of delinquency has been mailed by the Secretary of State, and shall advise the limited liability company of its right to request relief from the Secretary of State because of reasonable cause or unusual circumstances that justify such failure to file. If, within 60 days after providing notice of the delinquency, a statement pursuant to Section 17702.09 has not been filed by the limited liability company, the Secretary of State shall certify the name of such limited liability company to the Franchise Tax Board.

(b) Upon certification pursuant to subdivision (a), the Franchise Tax Board shall assess against the limited liability company the penalty provided in Section 19141 of the Revenue and Taxation Code.

(c) The penalty provided by Section 19141 of the Revenue and Taxation Code shall not apply to a limited liability company that on or prior to the date of certification pursuant to subdivision (a) has been canceled, has been merged into another limited liability company, other business entity, foreign other business entity, or foreign limited liability company, or has converted into another foreign business entity, foreign other business entity, or foreign limited liability company.

(d) The penalty herein provided shall not apply and the Secretary of State need not provide notice of the delinquency to a limited liability company the powers, rights, and privileges of which have been suspended by the Franchise Tax Board pursuant to Section 23301, 23301.5, or 23775 of the Revenue and Taxation Code on or prior to, and remain suspended on, the last day of the filing period pursuant to Section 17702.09. The Secretary of State need not provide notice of the filing requirement pursuant to Section 17702.09 to a limited liability company the powers, rights, and privileges of which have been so suspended by the Franchise Tax Board on or prior to, and remain suspended on, the day the Secretary of State prepares the notice for sending.

(e) If, after certification pursuant to subdivision (a) the Secretary of State finds (1) the required statement was filed or the required fee was paid before the expiration of the 60-day period after providing notice of the delinquency, or (2) the failure to provide notice of delinquency was due to an error of the Secretary of State, the Secretary of State shall promptly decertify the name of the limited liability company to the Franchise Tax Board. The Franchise Tax Board shall then promptly abate any

ARTICLE 13. Miscellaneous Provisions [17713.01 - 17713.13]

penalty assessed against the limited liability company pursuant to Section 19141 of the Revenue and Taxation Code.

(f) If the Secretary of State determines that the failure of a limited liability company to file the statement required by Section 17702.09 is excusable because of reasonable cause or unusual circumstances that justify such failure, the Secretary of State may waive the penalty imposed by this section and by Section 19141 of the Revenue and Taxation Code, in which case the Secretary of State shall not certify the name of the limited liability company to the Franchise Tax Board, or if already certified, the Secretary of State shall promptly decertify the name of the limited liability company.

(Added by Stats. 2012, Ch. 419, Sec. 20. Effective January 1, 2013. Operative January 1, 2014, by Sec. 32 of Ch. 419.)

17713.10.

(a) A limited liability company that (1) fails to file a statement pursuant to Section 17702.09 for an applicable filing period, (2) has not filed a statement pursuant to Section 17702.09 during the preceding 24 months, and (3) was certified for penalty pursuant to Section 17713.09 for the same filing period, shall be subject to suspension pursuant to this section rather than to penalty pursuant to Section 17713.09.

(b) When subdivision (a) is applicable, the Secretary of State shall notify the limited liability company that its powers, rights, and privileges will be suspended after 60 days if it fails to file a statement pursuant to Section 17702.09.

(c) After the expiration of the 60-day period without any statement filed pursuant to Section 17702.09, the Secretary of State shall notify the Franchise Tax Board of the suspension, and shall provide a notice of the suspension to the limited liability company and thereupon, except for the purpose of amending the articles of organization to set forth a new name, the powers, rights, and privileges of the limited liability company are suspended.

(d) A statement pursuant to Section 17702.09 may be filed notwithstanding suspension of the powers, rights, and privileges pursuant to this section or Section 23301 or 23301.5 of the Revenue and Taxation Code. Upon the filing of a statement pursuant to Section 17702.09 by a limited liability company that has suffered suspension pursuant to this section, the Secretary of State shall certify that fact to the Franchise Tax Board and the limited liability company may thereupon be relieved from suspension unless the limited liability company is held in suspension by the Franchise Tax Board by reason of Section 23301 or 23301.5 of the Revenue and Taxation Code.

(Added by Stats. 2012, Ch. 419, Sec. 20. Effective January 1, 2013. Operative January 1, 2014, by Sec. 32 of Ch. 419.)

17713.11.

(a) Sections 17713.09 and 17713.10 apply to foreign limited liability companies with respect to the statements required to be filed by Section 17702.09. For this purpose, the suspension of the powers, rights, and privileges of a domestic limited liability company shall mean the forfeiture of the exercise of the powers, rights, and privileges of a foreign limited liability company in this state.
(b) The forfeiture of the exercise of the powers, rights, and privileges of a foreign limited liability company in this state as used in subdivision (a) does not prohibit the transaction of business in this state by a foreign limited liability company if the business transacted subsequent to the forfeiture would not, considered as an entirety, require the foreign limited liability company to obtain a certificate of registration pursuant to Section 17708.02.

(Added by Stats. 2012, Ch. 419, Sec. 20. Effective January 1, 2013. Operative January 1, 2014, by Sec. 32 of Ch. 419.)

17713.12.

(a) A limited liability company is liable for a civil penalty in an amount not exceeding one million dollars ($1,000,000) if the limited liability company does both of the following:
   (1) Has actual knowledge that a member, officer, manager, or agent of the limited liability company does any of the following:
      (A) Makes, publishes, or posts, or has made, published, or posted, either generally or privately to the shareholders or other persons, either of the following:
         (i) An oral, written, or electronically transmitted report, exhibit, notice, or statement of its affairs or pecuniary condition that contains a material statement or omission that is false and intended to give membership shares in the limited liability company a materially greater or a materially less apparent market value than they really possess.
         (ii) An oral, written, or electronically transmitted report, prospectus, account, or statement of operations, values, business, profits, or expenditures that includes a material false statement or omission intended to give membership shares in the limited liability company a materially greater or a materially less apparent market value than they really possess.
      (B) Refuses or has refused to make any book entry or post any notice required by law in the manner required by law.
      (C) Misstates or conceals or has misstated or concealed from a regulatory body a material fact in order to deceive a regulatory body to avoid a statutory or regulatory duty, or to avoid a statutory or regulatory limit or prohibition.
   (2) Within 30 days after actual knowledge is acquired of the actions described in paragraph (1), the limited liability company knowingly fails to do both of the following:

ARTICLE 13. Miscellaneous Provisions [17713.01 - 17713.13]

      (A) Notify the Attorney General or appropriate government agency in writing, unless the limited liability company has actual knowledge that the Attorney General or appropriate government agency has been notified.

      (B) Notify its members and investors in writing, unless the limited liability company has actual knowledge that the members and investors have been notified.

(b) The requirement for notification under this section is not applicable if the action taken or about to be taken by the limited liability company, or by a member, officer, manager, or agent of the limited liability company under paragraph (1) of subdivision (a), is abated within the time prescribed for reporting, unless the appropriate government agency requires disclosure by regulation.

(c) If the action reported to the Attorney General pursuant to this section implicates the government authority of an agency other than the Attorney General, the Attorney General shall promptly forward the written notice to that agency.

(d) If the Attorney General was not notified pursuant to subparagraph (A) of paragraph (2) of subdivision (a), but the limited liability company reasonably and in good faith believed that it had complied with the notification requirements of this section by notifying a government agency listed in paragraph (5) of subdivision (e), no penalties shall apply.

(e) For purposes of this section:

  (1) "Manager" means a person defined by subdivision (m) of Section 17701.01 having both of the following:

      (A) Management authority over the limited liability company.

      (B) Significant responsibility for an aspect of the limited liability company that includes actual authority for the financial operations or financial transactions of the limited liability company.

  (2) "Agent" means a person or entity authorized by the limited liability company to make representations to the public about the limited liability company's financial condition and who is acting within the scope of the agency when the representations are made.

  (3) "Member" means a person as defined by subdivision (o) of Section 17701.01 that is a member of the limited liability company at the time the disclosure is required pursuant to subparagraph (B) of paragraph (2) of subdivision (a).

  (4) "Notify its members" means to give sufficient description of an action taken or about to be taken that would constitute acts or omissions as described in paragraph (1) of subdivision (a). A notice or report filed by a limited liability company with the United States Securities and Exchange Commission that relates to the facts and circumstances giving rise to an obligation under paragraph (1) of subdivision (a) shall satisfy all notice requirements arising under paragraph (2) of subdivision (a) but shall not be the exclusive means of satisfying the notice requirements, provided that the Attorney General or appropriate agency is informed in writing that the filing has been made together with a copy of the filing or an electronic link where it is available online without charge.

(5) "Appropriate government agency" means an agency on the following list that has regulatory authority with respect to the financial operations of a limited liability company:
   (A) Department of Corporations.
   (B) Department of Insurance.
   (C) Department of Financial Institutions.
   (D) Department of Managed Health Care.
   (E) United States Securities and Exchange Commission.
(6) "Actual knowledge of the limited liability company" means the knowledge a member, officer, or manager of a limited liability company actually possesses or does not consciously avoid possessing, based on an evaluation of information provided pursuant to the limited liability company's disclosure controls and procedures.
(7) "Refuse to make a book entry" means the intentional decision not to record an accounting transaction when all of the following conditions are satisfied:
   (A) The independent auditors required recordation of an accounting transaction during the course of an audit.
   (B) The audit committee of the limited liability company has not approved the independent auditor's recommendation.
   (C) The decision is made for the primary purpose of rendering the financial statements materially false or misleading.
(8) "Refuse to post any notice required by law" means an intentional decision not to post a notice required by law when all of the following conditions exist:
   (A) The decision not to post the notice has not been approved by the limited liability company's audit committee.
   (B) The decision is intended to give the membership shares in the limited liability company a materially greater or a materially less apparent market value than they really possess.
(9) "Misstate or conceal material facts from a regulatory body" means an intentional decision not to disclose material facts when all of the following conditions exist:
   (A) The decision not to disclose material facts has not been approved by the limited liability company's audit committee.
   (B) The decision is intended to give the membership shares in the limited liability company a materially greater or a materially less apparent market value than they really possess.
(10) "Material false statement or omission" means an untrue statement of material fact or an omission to state a material fact necessary in order to make the statements made under the circumstances under which they were made not misleading.
(11) "Officer" means a person appointed pursuant to Section 17703.02, except an officer of a specified subsidiary limited liability company who is not also an officer of the parent limited liability company.
(f) This section only applies to limited liability companies that are issuers, as defined in Section 2 of the federal Sarbanes-Oxley Act of 2002 (15 U.S.C. Sec. 7201 et seq.).

(g) An action to enforce this section may only be brought by the Attorney General or a district attorney or city attorney in the name of the people of the State of California.

(Added by Stats. 2012, Ch. 419, Sec. 20. Effective January 1, 2013. Operative January 1, 2014, by Sec. 32 of Ch. 419.)

17713.13.

This title shall become operative on January 1, 2014.

(Added by Stats. 2012, Ch. 419, Sec. 20. Effective January 1, 2013. Operative January 1, 2014, by Sec. 32 of Ch. 419.)

www.ingramcontent.com/pod-product-compliance
Lightning Source LLC
Chambersburg PA
CBHW051735170526
45167CB00002B/944